6/7

D0935364

The Difficulty of Being

JEAN COCTEAU

The Difficulty of Being

INTRODUCTION BY NED ROREM

Translated by Elizabeth Sprigge

Coward-McCann, Inc. New York

Translated from the French
La Difficulté d'Etre

This translation is dedicated to the memory of
KATRIONA SPRIGGE
whose unfailing interest sustained me
during 'la difficulté de traduire'
—Elizabeth Sprigge

I'D TAKE THE FIRE
(*A Souvenir of Jean*)
BY
NED ROREM

"Je sens une difficulté d'être." Thus did Fontenelle, the centenarian, reply when he was dying and his doctor asked: "M. Fontenelle, what do you feel?" Only his belonged to his last hour. Mine has been from the beginning.

— *On being without being*

One rainy afternoon in 1951 during my first visit to the meridional château of the remarkable Vicomtesse de Noailles (she who had commissioned "The Blood of a Poet"), I found on her shelves a ragged first edition of the book you now hold. Beneath its disturbing title the author had autographed a medieval sleeve from which emerged gaunt fingers clutching a plume, bewitched and still moving in that famous starry scrawl: *Chère amie, comment vous dédicacer un tel livre!*—"How inscribe such a book to you!" The charitable implication that she too shared his seeming ease for such beauty as distinguishes an artist from his fellow man is perhaps what led the Vicomtesse lately to declare of her childhood: "I was Jean's Lolita."

We all felt that, even before we knew him. Authors we love we "relate" to, we think we'd get on with them, yearn for their living contact. Jean Cocteau's literary humanity provoked this yearning more than any other artist of our time. As unsolved crimes are often confessed to by innocent old ladies, or as New York bars still harbor septuagenarians who swear they are "layers" of Djuna Barnes' model for Doctor O'Conner, so the city of Paris once swarmed with siblings claiming to be the original *enfants terribles* from whom their fabulous friend had fired a masterpiece. Such claims are usually unproductive and always fallacious: "People do not read but read themselves." After the fact and by association the models base themselves on the masterpiece, forgetting that a writer is only a writer when he's writing—that "awake" he's as ordinary as anyone.

Except Cocteau! He early learned from his junior Radiguet that an artist by definition cannot be ordinary, that he has only therefore to write like others to appear extraordinary. And the extraordinary oozed like ectoplasm into his waking hours too; to meet him—however briefly—was indeed to know him, to be momentarily endowed with his *ease of beauty*.

The ease of beauty. But at what a price—ease is so hard! All in the end is resolved except the enigma of existence ("It must be a dream that one can live at ease in one's own skin"), though from the poet's bloody plume the attempted resolution itself shapes art, art with its urgent imperfections, for beauty limps.

I mulled the yellowing leaves of this book until the rain had cleared into an April sunset, by which time I sensed a new contact with the *flesh* of the man (for the man in person was contradictorily a *skeleton* of his product), recalling how I too had first come to know him, to *want* to know him. In Chicago, aged thirteen, David Sachs, not without malice, lent me those novels which were to pervade my thinking as insidiously as Huymans' pervaded that of Dorian Gray. The next few years produced for those of our milieu the gospel of Cocteau's first three movies. And he knew then what now we've come to know: that films, not the stage, are such stuff as dreams will all be made on. His dream of "Beauty and the Beast" he brought himself to America in 1948, when we all went to examine him at a Gotham Book Mart cocktail. (He arrived very late. Where had he been? In Harlem, it seems, to find an impecunious old friend, the former world champion Al Brown.) With Paul Goodman as makeshift translator (we knew French then, but not how to talk it) we applauded the verbal acrobatics of our current world champion, who then bowed himself out of the shop and into the night of his new Manhattan, which suddenly we too found rich and strange. He led us to our own water—a fountain of youth—and showed us how to drink.

I cannot know whether his Catholic way of drinking, rather than the Quaker romanticism of my infancy, turned me into a Frenchman rather than a German (we are all culturally one or the other), but it did lead me to Paris, which became a second home where I would risk the dangers of disillusion by encountering unsuspected aspects of a legend. Only presumption could claim my reportage now as singular, as more qualified than another's, as "truth"— though at least my truth is my own and I long to share it. That's just the point: Cocteau's very nature (nature or magic?) impels preemption in his fans.

Thus it was that six months previous to the wet April day of which I speak—on October 6, 1950, to be precise— I first visited the skeleton in the flesh.

"You yourself must find a way to meet me—miracles work better than appointments," was his challenge to my letter. Human intercourse was for him a game but the rules were easily learned. I "found a way" and we made a date. Then I panicked. You don't *meet* idols, they don't exist on mortal terms. Jean-the-Artist had spellbound three European generations: Diaghilev's demand "astound me" unleashed in 1912 a talent which, until the last war's end, had dazzled every class with its ballets and monologues, movies and plays, its novels and essays, poems and paintings, even its choreography (if as a musician Cocteau lacked a voice, he compensated by "inventing" Satie and the *Groupe des Six*). Jean-the-Man had been no less formidable: had he not inherited from Wilde the title of "the world's most brilliant talker"? and from De Quincey that of the world's most conspicuous *opiomane?* —was he not haunted by the melancholy suicides of so many whose strength was unequal to his?—had not *Le Livre Blanc* described his parties in Toulon brothels? —had he not attended operas with Barbette, the Texan trapezist in drag? —and created and destroyed names now more legendary than his own? —had not Gide monumentalized him (if dubiously) as Passavant in *The Counterfeiters?* —and Freud himself dissected his *Sang d'un Poète?* If to a Continental admirer the image of Cocteau was awesome, how much more so was the fact to a young American weaned on the glamorous Eternal Return!

It was eleven o'clock of a perfect morning. He himself welcomed me into his small apartment overlooking those gray gardens harboring hordes of screeching children, long rows of chestnut trees, and the expensive Véfour restaurant. After telling the housekeeper not to disturb us until one, the *maître* followed me into a tiny red room and locked the door. The red room contained a tiny crimson bed heaped with recent art reviews (all had uncut pages), a telegraph set (out of order), a ceiling-high blackboard displaying a boy's scarlet chalk profile, a Siamese cat (female), and a pervading heady fragrance (opium maybe). Through his window echoed the real world, laughing games and fountains plashing, and across the courtyard I recognized the yellow blinds of Colette's casements. (But he has described it all in this very book: *On the Palais-Royal.*)

Tall thin Cocteau seemed agitated, explained he'd come home only minutes before I rang, had been to check up on *le père Gide,* from whom he'd gotten a *pneumatique* in a disquieting handwriting. I was impressed that he had nonetheless found time to don a floor-length azure robe. The long sleeves hid his hands, though in reinforcing each *bon mot* (three a minute) he pointed skyward and the famous fingers shot forth like antennae. Like antennae too were his great ears, his rebellious kinky hair, even his voice, which listened while it spoke in a timbre unrelated to the one we knew from records—higher, less mundane, more insistent.

Insistent it was as he incessantly moved, never sitting, a
jittery jaguar forever pacing, occasionally petting the sister
Siamese in passing, talking, talking in phrases that bristled
with *con* and *emmerder* ripe as forbidden fruit to my
would-be obstreperous but puritan taste. Yet his congested atmosphere seemed all elegance without the crumbling corners
one finds in even the richest old French homes. For my host
was young. Desperately.

At no time did I sense the lazy-hot mystery which proved
so fatal to Maurice Sachs and others here in former decades.
Nor did I find him beautiful. He did strike me as—well—
more *engagé* than I'd have guessed, for France in those days
swarmed with his tired replica. Now here was the real thing,
and oh, what posture! what thin lips releasing from the true
source such a thick sheen of verbs! My own talk was reticent,
but since he ended all phrases with a brutal *quoi!* or *hein!*
I couldn't not reply. My dull answers he shined up with
his own tongue, then spit them like sparks back into my
dazed features, while paradoxically putting me at ease, *including* me.

"We must know what we're doing, we poets, and know
well, even if not why. Remain comrades . . . They call
me robber. But of course! They're right for the wrong reasons, *ces cons-là!* Poetry comes from elsewhere, an uninvited
guest. Doesn't your music? That music, those poems themselves steal from *us* . . . They call me liar. Aren't beautiful lies what all children know as fairy tales? Certainly each
child lies; but when he succeeds in revamping his lie as
personal expression—why he becomes immense, *quoi!* Do
you not do the same? . . . Art's not on a page, not in the
concert hall, or at least not *only*. It's a snake, a river, a
vine twisting all over from high to low, shrinking in its
growth, expanding to become anyone's little perilous property. Listen! say listen there, come to the window! Hear
that *ouvrier* down there? He's whistling the bassoon solo
from the *Sacre*. It belongs to *him* now! [The tune in fact
was *La Vie en Rose*, which in any case would have proved
his point.] Kinsey interviewed you? Really? We French,

you know, are more amused than intrigued by your charts and lists, by your slow psychoanalysis—*that* we've had, known, used, abandoned. We don't specialize like you, but scatter our seed—*si j'ose dire*—to inseminate all manner of fauna, *hein!* Yet he's right, your Kinsey, to request genital data from his worried clients. Everything counts in a man—*et je ne crois guère aux hommes de petite verge . . .* My voice, you say, sounds like whose? like Yves Salgues'? You hear him through me but uttering different things and grow confused? *Mon pauvre ami.* We too were confused, but poets: making order in the form of disorder, aristocrats with the faces of anarchists. But oh, today! you . . ."

I had no reason to think that the same disc might not be put on for the next tourist who came knocking (and what of it?). I do remember that he gave of himself with more immediacy than I've ever known. Yet he warns us in these pages that "to receive all the callers in despair is impossible . . . Let us beware of the drowning who cling to us and who drown us." Perhaps because precisely I was not drowning (not yet) I could grasp his coherence of the unrelated, could comprehend what people meant by his encounter and friendship being one. Like our Frank O'Hara he gave himself promiscuously in speech, a lover without contact—which is to say without ulterior motive. This violent lack of motive is rare and hypnotic. Cocteau's sorcery was in sympathy, a sympathy of perceptive monologuing which caused even fools to feel a fair exchange. So he swayed millions, wholesomely or injuriously, depending on who could keep that unalterable pace which he maintained went faster than beauty and converted the ordinary into works of art.

The "ordinary" that morning grew from talk of passion and crime in American towns, into procedures of so-called creation and the creator's social location. His verb for the creative act was *chier* ("*Quand j'ai chié mon Orphée!*"). "Artists must stay put, grow ever more selfish, never seek to rearrange the world. They must—and from the start, as I have—create and live by their own mythology, discovering

for its expression the mystic force hidden within the rough
state [*l'état brut*] of the medium itself—the bronze, the
words, the notes, whatever—all these lead a life of their own
and lead us with them, as mathematicians are led, are mag-
netized, by the more-than-human power of numbers. Artists
must because they have no choice but to be exorcised only
to be reenslaved."

Cocteau's words, like nature, were an overflow, an *em-
barras de richesses* from which his work was ultimately
tailored with the economy of a diamond cutter. He was
nevertheless not so uneconomical as to avoid looking at his
watch. Suddenly my two hours were gone.

A warm *au revoir* sent me off through the children's garden, passing beneath Colette's window, to have lunch alone
—not at the Véfour but in a bistrot across the Seine. There
I pondered the verb *to know well* which, after all, has little
to do with longevity or habit, but with intensity and exchange. Because I was feeling—buoyantly, if gullibly—that on
that autumn noon I had made a friend.

In September of 1963 he mailed me what may have been
his final drawing, a sketch I'd requested to illustrate my
setting of Elizabeth Bishop's *Visits to St. Elizabeths.* His
accompanying letter was signed:*"Avec la tendresse fidèle d'un
pauvre malade dont la convalescence sera très lourde et très
longue* [with the faithful tenderness of a poor sick man
whose convalescence will be heavy and very long]." Two
weeks later he died. Maybe that little fortnight was indeed
très longue. In any event I found his handwriting (and he
always wrote by hand, in a script as carnavalesque as his
oratory) now as disquieting as he had found Gide's thirteen
years earlier—and as my own may be found sooner than I
think.

During those thirteen years we engaged in regular correspondence, his side including always one of those drawings
with which he was so lavish, or a book of new poems
"thrown to the sea like a bottle containing my gentlest
thoughts." And we were to meet again a dozen times, at

Hervé Dugardin's or Marie Laure's, at the Auric's or *chez les duchesses,* at backstage brawls or noble picnics. For his life glared socially as it did industriously, and everywhere he set the tone. Or hoped he did. The fact was that after forty virtuosic years his prestige (not to mention his productive vitality) was in decline, at least for youth, which comprises that public most needed by aging geniuses. But youth's needs were elsewhere. Not too slowly but all too surely French *fantaisistes* and poets were being replaced by artistic philosophers and practical proselytizers.

Cocteau's sleight-of-hand had for a while dissembled a lack of discrimination. More than anyone else he combined the sublimely right with the unutterably trashy. Who else could so wonderfully announce, "One must know how to go too far" (he later credited this quip—though not publicly—to Péguy), and then pervert himself in an official address to Marlene Dietrich, "Madame, your name starts with a caress and ends in a whiplash!"? Who else could summon tears so purging (although Stravinsky now finds them bathetic) as those implied at the end of *Oedipus Rex,* "Farewell, we loved you," and the next day accept a sum from a stocking manufacturer for the slogan: "Ladies, your limbs are poems: bind them in our hose"? If in the twenties he promoted such diverse talents as Braque and the Fratellini Brothers, in the thirties Jean Marais and Edith Piaf, and in the forties Jean Genêt and Maurice Gendron—he endorsed with equal vim a series of mediocrities.

All this was valid, fun, fruitful, indeed quite like the non-specialist Frenchmen whose "inspired Jean" outdid them all as Renaissance Man. But with World War II and the advent of Existentialism his wand lost its power—he waved and no one looked. Enthusiasm alone couldn't hold the stage, and novelty changes meaning when years roll by, as a star changes meaning when telescopes approach. Cocteau's star—the signature that was his heart—dimmed drastically in 1953. He lay near death for weeks and was already mourned by *les vieux petits amis.* He had been struck by that same stone snowball that literally broke two of his heroes' hearts

—"the marble fist blow which brings beauty, quick to the heart, in passing." But he performed a new miracle by recovering. This time everyone looked as he secured for himself that most coveted of cultural thrones, a chair in the French Academy. Such an honor had been systematically denied all "unconventional" authors from Baudelaire to Sartre.

Being thus immortalized in life, Cocteau, as though by agreement with the angel of his mythology, suffered another slump. Officially a great man, his last ten years produced little of apparent consequence beyond two excellent books of poems and one fair movie. He did make of his protégé a legal heir (at present under dispute), allow himself to be pictured cutting capers with Chaplin or Picasso, and appear at concerts to boo or cheer, when booing and cheering no longer of themselves proved much. He did, also, contribute prefaces and blurbs (less influential now than Sartre's) and continue until the end in the practice of generous acquaintanceship. But his stylish rage and vigor were collapsing. Finally, the eleventh of October, 1963, on learning of the premature death of his old friend Edith Piaf, he too died—from pure sympathy, one almost feels—at his country home in Milly, uttering the strangely bland (for him) epigram: "The ship is going down."

If a dying artist has the consolation that his works may live on, the terrible question arises: which ones? That Cocteau should quit this earth in hand with Piaf seemed to us then a final homage to the art of love; today, with the irony of perspective, it looks like a classical bit of upstaging. For the theater was Cocteau's most telling milieu, and whether or not he created directly for it, his whole output, including his daily life, was essentially dramatic. It seems unlikely, however, that his professional collaborations with the rare Edith in 1940 stand much chance of survival except as exercises in jargon. *Le Fantôme de Marseille*, about a woman whose sweetheart is murdered while masquerading *en travestie*, and particularly *Le Bel Indifférent*, about the same woman with a mute lover, now read like tryouts for

the superb *Voix Humaine,* which remains a masterpiece
both in its original black and white version, and in the en-
suing heartbreaking technicolor of Poulenc. Basically theatrical are his nine movies, from *Le Sang d'un Poète* to
Orphée, and also of course his fifteen odd stage works, from
Antigone through *Bacchus*—not to mention lesser monologues for Berthe Bovy and Marianne Oswald, or ballets for
Massine and Babilée. But theatrical too (by which I mean
visual, kinetic—given to move, literally, the beholder) are
his introspective verses, from the very early *Vocabulaire* to
his late *Claire-Obscure,* and even his criticism, from those
first early "notes about music" (*Le Coq et l'Arlequin*) in
1918 to *La Démarche d'un Poète,* 1953.

And so, finally, are these "objective" essays which, with
their sequel, *Journal d'un Inconnu,* constitute a series one
might term Dramatic Abstractions on such diversities as his
own body, frivolity, youth, France, dreams, customs, or reading. But he was a poet, a painter, and a child as well, and
blended the three.

Like all true poets he anticipates science when speaking
here of, say, pain. (As to whether—as he maintains—he actually wrote of pain while in pain is as irrelevant as in his
Opium. One does not, for example, write about mescalin
while under it; you can't do two things at once: feel pain
and objectify the feeling. What *is* relevant is that he makes
us feel it.)

Like all true painters he confronts his witness with an
animate object when dealing with, say, death. He shows
what it is like *to wake up dead!* His continual obsession
with mirrors taught us that they are the doors through
which death comes and goes. ("Look at yourself all your
life in the mirror and you'll see Death working like bees
in a glass hive.")

Like all true children he finds good in evil when talking,
say, of haunted houses, as he does here in a piece called
just that, or in his skit *La Farce du Château.* ("They imitate us and only offer us what we give them. But this echo
speaks and insists on dialogue.")

His own haunted house was formed from transparent

stained glass of the queerest hues, although his domesticity was never—except by allusion—a subject for his prose as it was for the otherwise more circumspect Gide. Perhaps the present volume comes closer than others to revealing a bare heart, yet the revelations no sooner advance than they recede in waves of tantalizing generality. ("I dare not confess here, even though I am resolved to tell all . . ."; ". . . it is not just a defense mechanism against sickness which forces me to write this particular book.") Finally the waves freeze into essays as succinct as those of Bacon or Hazlitt, if more compassionate.

For compassionate he was, and, like any artist, utterly vulnerable, but vulnerable *with tact*. By all this I mean that personal sexuality (except in the pseudonymous *Livre Blanc* or various unsigned illustrations for Genêt) was never his professional theme, though God knows it was often a send-off—as with most intellectuals—for blooming conversation.

Conversation, until 1950, was an art and a pleasure, and Jean was France's chief professor of it. Surrounded, always surrounded he was, like Andy Warhol now, by leeches and aspirers and—who knows?—genius (though could Malanga be compared to Radiguet?); yet where Warhol is mute Cocteau was eloquent. At the start he too surrounded (if one person can be said to surround), learning, learning with listening eye and watchful ear. As sensitive to the verb as his predecessor Anna de Noailles, and to nature as his neighbor Colette herself, he tells of conversations with microbes and the very thoughts of plants (see *On Laughter, On Beauty*). Where McLuhan today promotes a touching if clumsy faith in the artist as the only one "who knows," Cocteau yesterday, *being* an artist, spoke with truth that was more than truth of poets "who commit themselves for no other reason than to lose."

Yet three generations had stylishly misrepresented Cocteau as at worst a liar, at best a conjurer (how impatient he was with that word!). Perhaps I too have so misrepresented him in the foregoing. Yet he *was* a conjurer in that, as the serious thinker he has proven himself to be, he converted impossibly sluggish minds into poetic participants. And he *was* a liar in that, as he pointed out, his were "true lies," and he borrowed plots (as did Shakespeare) indiscriminately. Certainly his *Eternel Retour* or *Les Parents Terribles* are no closer in intention to Tristan or the so-called Boulevard Comedies than are, for instance, Albee's *Zoo Story* to *The Blue Hotel* of Stephen Crane, or James' *Roderick Hudson* to *La Peau de Chagrin* of Balzac.

But three generations also hailed Cocteau as a prophet. Are not his initials, after all, those of Jesus? and his trademark the Star of Bethlehem flashing like a flying saucer? And if that flash now sometimes illuminates the *démodé*, at its keenest it pierces like a laser beam straight into the human heart and moves it as no Gallic philosopher has moved it since. Cocteau's curiosity about all matters, at home and abroad and in the cosmos, was healthily untypical of his countrymen so drably self-confined within their frontiers.

This hearty motion, then, will possibly have been Cocteau's lasting contribution. And not, curiously (at least for me), as exemplified in the plays, but in the two strange novels, *Thomas l'Imposteur* and *Les Enfants Terribles*, wherein the author's recurring theme of fatality hits hardest.

Despite a tardy if vague awakening, France, with her blindness to outside energy and adherence to national tradition, has grown increasingly moribund in fancy. This has never seemed more true than today when so many of her principal spokesmen are left unreplaced in death. Cocteau had invented a France of his own, then invited others to wax and shimmer among his magic flames which colored every aspect of the land where now only an afterglow remains.

That country adores categoric generalities. A literary monthly once posed this familiar question to several writers: If your house were burning down and you could take away one thing, what would it be? "I'd take the fire," answered Jean Cocteau. And he did.

N. R. 1966

The Difficulty of Being

Contents

Foreword

I regret the telling of too many things that are there to tell and too few of those that are not there to tell but which come back to us, so completely surrounded by emptiness that we no longer know if it was a train, or which one, that carried the bicycles in the van – but why, in God's name? – since the market-place (and I'm thinking of the one at Saint-Rémy-sur-Deule or of Cadet Rouselle[1] or of any other place of grimy slate) was on a sheer slope ending at that accursed house – or maybe not – where we lunched, guilty of what and with whom, I ask myself. There is enough to let me remember this and the steeply sloping *place* in the sun, but not enough for me to recall the date, the name, the region, the people, the details. All of which places this *place*, a regular sun-trap, in such precarious balance that I feel sick at the thought of it still existing in space with that low house and those people down below.

And other things not to tell. Such as about a village fair where I got lost, on the other side of the Seine at Sartrouville

---

[1] The simple-minded hero of an old popular song, symbolizing anything ramshackle or nonsensical. E.S.

perhaps, near a laundry-boat on which was written : *Madame Levaneur*. There they smoked cacao-leaf cigars. And those cigars, those too, have nothing to do with anything sober or human like the Académie française or the Post Office.

Then too a shawl over my head and the vast coolness of the glacier, and the name Interlaken, and the flower edelweiss and the jerking funicular that starts at the bottom with iced beer, a volley of shot right into one's temples, and ends at the top in a glass structure, with cyclamen, yellow butterflies, and clerics who chloroform them and crucify them on cork.

Another thing. Well, as for this, I no longer know in what life, and it was certainly not in a dream. (At least one knows where dream things are : in the dream.) A young chimney-sweep in a top hat, on a bone-shaker, with the elegance of an acrobat of extraordinary versatility, capable of scaling the ladder he is carrying on his back like a musical instrument. This was near a noisy saw-mill. And others, others, others. And from the emptiness the wreck of derelict emotions flowing in on the scum and returning to the open sea.

So there it is. This is how it strikes me in the peace of this countryside, of this house that cherishes me, that I live in alone, in this March of 1947, after a long, long wait.

I could weep. Not for my house nor for having had to wait for it. At having told too many things that were there to be told and too few of those that were not there to tell.

In the end, everything is resolved, except the difficulty of being, which is never resolved.

Milly, March 1947

On conversation

I have passed the half-century. That is to say that death should not have very far to go before catching up with me. The comedy is well on its way. There are few cues left to me. If I look around (at what relates to me) I find nothing but legends thick as leaves on the ground. I avoid getting involved and being caught in this snare. But, except for Roger Lannes' preface to Seghers' *Morceaux choisis* I find nothing of myself (nothing, that is to say, that reveals my face). Neither in praise nor in censure do I find the slightest attempt to disentangle the true from the false.

It is true that I can find excuses for the silence of those who could unravel threads. My hair has always grown in all directions and my teeth too and my beard. My nerves and my soul must surely grow in the same way. That is what makes me incomprehensible to those who grow all in one direction and are incapable of imagining a hay-stack. It is this that baffles those who could rid me of this legendary leprosy. They do not know how to take me.

This organic disorder is a safeguard for me because it keeps the thoughtless at a distance. I also get certain advantages from it. It gives me diversity, contrast, a quickness in leaning to one side or the other, as this or that object invites me, and in regaining my balance.

Certainly it makes my dogma obscure, my cause difficult to defend. But since no one comes to my aid, I run to my own and try to keep up with myself.

For the last five months I have been directing my film *La Belle et la Bête* in a deplorable state of health. After a bad bout of sunstroke in the Bassin d'Arcachon, my life has been a ceaseless struggle with germs and the havoc they cause to one's constitution.

I am writing these lines on a mountain of snow surrounded by other mountains, beneath a sullen sky. Medicine asserts that germs surrender to altitude. It seems to me that, on the contrary, they love it and gain strength here at the same time as I do.

Suffering is a habit. I am inured to it. During the film they talked about my courage. I would call it rather a laziness in looking after myself. I let myself sink as heavily as possible, with a passive strength, into work.

This work distracted me from my illness and as it was clear that the snow treatment was useless, I found it more profitable to keep doggedly to my work than to seek exile in tedious solitude. Even here, where I should curb my spirit and live curled up in a ball, I never cease conversing with you.

With whom else should I converse? These hotels are the receptacles of a new society which lives at our expense and emulates a luxury learned from films and newspapers. As a result there is this hurly-burly of children galloping between the tables, whose families don't know that there is such a thing as being well brought up. In doorways the ladies give way to us. One recognizes here the usual method of showing the customer out of a very small shop. These ladies and gentlemen go about looking positively mediaeval in their sporting outfits. They put on their skis, climb slopes and proudly break their legs. I keep to myself as far as possible, walk in the snow, shut myself up in my room, and avenge myself on this piece of paper for not being able to give myself up to the only sport I like, which in 1580 was called conferring, and which is conversation.

Now the sun is out, painting our lovely world with many colours. Afar through my window this world shows me a pageant of knights on horseback, surrounded by pennants, lances, escutcheons, fanfares, hustings of a white tournament. The peaks are flecked with shadows and with snow more dazzling than scarlet. But I converse none the less, for my joy is no joy if I cannot share it with someone. At Morzine, I have no contact with anyone. These people scarcely have the power of speech. They only use their mouths for eating. Many leave, recalled by the business which gives them wealth.

On my childhood

I was born on the fifth of July 1889, Place Sully at Maisons-Laffitte (Seine-et-Oise).

Maisons-Laffitte is a kind of park for trainers, strewn with villas, gardens, avenues of limes, lawns, flower-beds, squares with fountains. There the race-horse and the bicycle reign supreme. One used to play tennis at this house or that, in a bourgeois world which the Dreyfus case split in two. The Seine, the training track, the wall of the forest of Saint-Germain into which you enter through a little gate, deserted corners in which to play detectives, the camp below, the little inns with their arbours, the village fair, the fireworks, the gallantry of the firemen, the Mansard château, its wild flowering grass and its busts of Roman emperors, all this made up a kingdom calculated to encourage the illusion childhood has of living in places unlike any others in the world.

Last year I had the painful experience of being taken by friends to that Place Sully, full of those pale green spikes that creep up inside one's sleeves and of wild pinks. I fondly thought that I would show them my house and perhaps, difficult though

this is, make them share the dream it conjures up for me. My
first feeling was of being lost in space, as happens when one
is blindfolded and released at one point when one thinks one is
at another. Was that my white gate, my trellised fence; were
those my trees, my lawn, the house where I was born and the
long windows of the billiard room? A sand track had replaced
grass, pond, flower-beds. A tall grey structure flanked by a barn
occupied the site of our house. Grooms came and went, looking
at us suspiciously as they passed. This produced in me, while I
held on to the bars of the repainted gate, *like a prisoner shut out,*
a painful sensation which was nothing more than my memories
being pitchforked away, unable to find their old ways and the
niche where I believed them to be sleeping until I came. I turned
round. Would I perhaps find a refuge on the other side of the
square? We used to cross it in the sunshine to go to the *clos*
André (so named after my uncle). The iron gate would creak
open and reveal on the right the pelts of heliotrope. And then
Eden opened. The kitchen garden of discoveries. For it is in
the shade of thickets of lilac, of red-currant bushes, of outhouses
that childhood seeks to understand the secrets of the grown-up
people's universe.

An even worse surprise awaited me. The close had been par-
celled out in lots. It was crowded with little workmen's houses
which appeared to be numberless. The grapes in their paper
bags, the hot-cheeked peaches, the hairy gooseberries which
burst in the mouth, the smell of the geraniums in the green-
house, the flagstones of the hen-run, on which the greengages
fell, splitting their heads and bleeding gold, the frogs in the
pond, dead in operatic attitudes with the hand on the heart,
all this magic became, in that minute, the ghost of one murdered,
asking for justice.

We visited avenues where there was less destruction than in
my square. Gardens and houses still so unchanged that I could
have dug up some object buried forty years before, when we
played at hidden treasure. We strolled along the boundary of the
park where Max Lebaudy (the little Sugar Manufacturer)
organized bullfights and washed his carriages in champagne.
You may imagine how such sights could excite the cruel

and adventurous spirit of children. In 1904 we used to prowl round that fence and try to scale it, standing on the saddles of our bicycles.

But enough of that. To be moved confuses the soul. One cannot convey these kinds of memories any more than the events of a dream. It is as well to remind oneself that everyone harbours such memories and does not impose them on us.

If I have complained for rather too long, it is because my memory, no longer having any fixed abode, has to carry its luggage with it. But I have quickly strapped my bags and I shall not speak of it again.

On my style

I am neither cheerful nor sad. But I can be completely the one or completely the other to excess. In conversation, if I am in good form, I forget the sorrows behind me, a pain I am suffering from, forget myself, so greatly do words intoxicate me and sweep ideas along with them. They come to me far better than in solitude and, often, to write an article is torture, whereas I can speak it without effort. This frenzy of speech gives an impression of a facility that I do not possess. For as soon as I hold myself in check, this facility gives way to arduous labour, the climbing of a hill that seems to me precipitous and interminable. Added to which is a superstitious fear of getting going, being always afraid of starting on the wrong tack. This induces a kind of laziness and is akin to what the psychiatrists call 'the agony of the act'. The white paper, the ink, the pen alarm me. I know that they are in league against my will to write. If I succeed in conquering them, then the engine warms up, the work drives me and my mind functions. But it is essential that I should interfere as little as possible; that I should almost doze over it. The slightest consciousness of this process stops it. And if

I want to get it going again, I have to wait until the machinery chooses, and not try to persuade it by some trick. That is why I do not use tables, which intimidate me and look too inviting. I write at any hour, on my knee. With drawing it is the same. I know very well how to fake a line, but that's not the real thing, and I only give birth to the true line when it so wishes.

My dreams are nearly always criticisms of my actions, so severe and so accurate that they could be a lesson to me. But unfortunately they caricature the very structure of my soul and discourage me rather than giving me the means to battle with myself. For no one knows his own weaknesses better than I, and if I happen to read some article attacking me, I feel that I could strike closer to the mark, that the steel would bury itself up to the hilt and there would be nothing left for me to do but fold up, hang out my tongue and fall on my knees in the arena.

One must not confuse intelligence, so adept at duping its man, with that other organ, seated we know not where, which informs us – irrevocably – of our limitations. No one can scale them. The effort would be seen through. It would further emphasize the narrow space accorded to our movements. It is through the power to revolve within this space that talent proves itself. Only thus can we progress. And each progress can only be of a moral kind, since each one of our ventures takes us unawares. We can count on nothing but integrity. Every trick leads to another. A blunder is preferable. The anonymous public boos at it, but forgives us. Tricks give themselves away in the long run. The public turns away with the blank expression of a woman who once loved but loves no longer.

That is why I took pains not to waste my strength at school. I correct carelessly, let a thousand faults pass, am lazy about rereading my work and only reread the idea. So long as what's to be said is said, it's all one to me. All the same I have my method. This consists in being quick, hard, economical in words, in unrhyming my prose, in taking aim regardless of style and hitting the bull's-eye at whatever cost.

Rereading my work in proper perspective I am ashamed only

of the trimmings. They harm us, because they distract from us.
The public loves them; it is blinded by them and ignores the
rest. I have heard Charles Chaplin deplore having left in his
film *The Gold Rush* that dance of the bread rolls for which
every spectator congratulates him. To him it is only a blot that
catches the eye. I have also heard him say (on the subject of
decorative style) that after a film he 'shakes the tree'. One
must only keep, he added, what sticks to the branches.

Often the decoration is not of one's own volition. It is the
result of a certain balance. For the public such balance has a
superficial charm which consoles them for not properly appreciat-
ing the basic matter. This is the case with Picasso. This complete
artist is made up of a man and a woman. In him terrible
domestic scenes take place. Never was so much crockery smashed.
In the end the man is always right and slams the door. But there
remains of the woman an elegance, an organic gentleness, a kind
of luxuriousness which gives an excuse to those who are afraid
of strength and cannot follow the man beyond the threshold.

On the work and the legend

To be gifted is to be lost, unless one sees clearly in time to level the slopes instead of sliding down them all.

How to conquer a gift should be the main study of anybody who recognizes one in himself. And such a study is a subtle matter if by ill luck one only becomes aware of it rather late. I have spent my life and am still doing so, opposing an ill-starred destiny. What a dance it has led me!

And what a complex matter it is to be clear-sighted, since gifts assume the first shape they meet and this shape might perchance be the right one. Mine was wrong. What saved me was that I went so badly astray that I could no longer have the slightest doubt.

My family was no help to me. It judged by success. It was amateur and meddlesome.

Raymond Radiguet, during the Great War (which he called the summer holidays) read, on the Marne at Parc Saint-Maur, the books in his father's library. They were ours. Thus we were his classics. We bored him stiff, as was only natural, and at the age of fourteen he longed to refute us. When I met him at Max

Jacob's, he pulled me out of a pitfall, for through fleeing from myself as fast as my legs would carry me, I was in danger of finding myself one day heaven knows where. He calmed me down with his own calm. He taught me the true way. That of forgetting that one is a poet and of allowing things to happen subconsciously. But his engine was new. Mine was carboned up and noisy.

At this time Raymond Radiguet was fifteen. Erik Satie was nearly sixty. Those two – at opposite ends of the pole – taught me to understand myself. The only glory of which I can boast is that I was amenable to their teaching. Erik Satie was an incredible character. By that I mean that one cannot describe him. Honfleur and Scotland were his paternal and maternal origins. It was from Honfleur he acquired the style of Alphonse Allais' stories, stories in which there is hidden poetry and which are quite unlike any of the silly anecdotes that go the rounds.

From Scotland he got a dour eccentricity.

In appearance he was a civil servant, with a goatee, an eye-glass, an umbrella, a bowler hat.

Egotistic, cruel, obsessive, he listened to nothing that did not subscribe to his dogma and flew into violent tempers with those who opposed it. Egotistic, because he thought of nothing but his music. Cruel, because he defended his music. Obsessive, because he went on polishing his music. And his music was tender. So was he, in his own way.

For several years Erik Satie came in the morning to 10 Rue d'Anjou and sat in my room. He kept on his overcoat (on which he could not have borne the slightest stain), his gloves, his hat tilted over his eyeglass, his umbrella in his hand. With his free hand he shielded his mouth, which would curl when he talked or laughed. He would come from Arcueil on foot. He lived there in a small room where, after his death, all the letters from his friends were found under a mountain of dust. He had not opened one.

He scrubbed himself with pumice stone. He never used water.

In that period, when music overflowed in all directions, acknowledging the genius of Debussy, fearing his despotism (they fraternized and quarrelled to the end), he turned his back on his school and became, at the *Schola Cantorum,* the comic Socrates we knew.

There he pumiced himself, he schooled himself, he filed himself down and forged the vessel and the small orifice through which his exquisite strength had only to flow freely.

Once free, he would make fun of himself, tease Ravel, and out of modesty give to the fine pieces played by Ricardo Viñes, droll titles calculated immediately to alienate many mediocre minds.

There you have the man. Certainly it would have been pleasanter to wallow in the waves of Wagner and of Debussy. But we had to have a rule of life, however obscure it may seem to you. Every age rejects some kinds of charm. Already in *le Coq et l'Arlequin* I denounced that of *Le Sacre.* And in rejecting himself Stravinsky was to outdo us all.

Erik Satie was my schoolmaster. Radiguet my examiner. Contact with them showed me my faults without their having to tell me of them, and if I was unable to correct them, at least I knew them.

To shape oneself is not easy. To reshape oneself still less so. Until *Les Mariés de la Tour Eiffel,* the first work in which I owed nothing to anybody, and which is unlike any other, in which I discovered my cypher, I forced the lock and twisted my key in every direction.

Orphée, l'Ange Heurtebise, Opéra saved me from such goings on. True, one soon falls into them again, and until that day when I succeeded in not involving myself in anything, I mean to say in only involving myself in what concerns me, I still found myself in tight corners.

My worst fault, like almost everything in me, springs from childhood. For I am still the victim of those unhealthy rites which make children obsessive, so that they arrange their plates in a certain way at meals and only step over certain grooves in the pavement.

In the midst of work, here are these symptoms gripping me, forcing me to resist what is driving me, involving me in strange halting writing, preventing me from saying what I want to say.

That is why my style often assumes an air of its own which I loathe, or else suddenly drops it. Inward cramps which reproduce those nervous peculiarities to which childhood abandons itself in secret and by which it believes it can exorcise fate.

Even now as I am explaining them, I experience them. I try to conquer them. I stumble against them, I get bogged down in them, I lose myself in them. I should like to break the spell. My obsession gets the better of me.

I may possibly flatter myself that I can give an outline to what I turn out, whereas so little am I able to do this that the very force which I turn out resists me and decides for itself even the shape of its outline.

That is my definition of the writing sickness from which I suffer and which makes me prefer conversation.

I have few words in my pen. I turn them over and over. The idea gallops ahead. When it stops and looks back, it sees me flagging behind. That puts it out of patience. It escapes. And it is lost for good.

I leave the paper. I busy myself with something else, I open my door. I am free. That's easily said. The idea returns at top speed and I plunge into work.

It is my passionate struggling against cramp that earns me a covering of legends, some more absurd than others. I am a man made invisible by fables and monstrously visible on account of this.

A course that sidetracks people soon wearies them. They grow tired of following us. They invent one for us and if we do not conform to this course, they bear us a grudge. It is too late for us to complain. We 'look fine', as they say. It is dangerous not to conform with people's image of us, because they do not readily retract their opinions.

It is along the way of one's escape that the legend grows and thrives.

If a foreign critic judges us, there is a good chance that he will hit the mark. He knows us better than our compatriots who flatten their noses against us. Here space plays the part of time. Our compatriots judge the work through the man. Seeing of the man nothing but a false image, their judgment is false.

It is, it seems, a social crime to desire solitude. After a piece of work, I flee. I seek new territory. I fear the slackness of habit. I want to be free of techniques, of experience – clumsy. That is to be a trifler, a traitor, an acrobat, a *fantaisiste*. To be complimentary : a magician.

A wave of the wand and the books are written, the film is shot, the pen draws, the play is staged. It is very simple. Magician. That word makes everything easy. No need to labour at our work. It all happens of its own accord.

On Raymond Radiguet

At my very first meeting with Raymond Radiguet I may say that I guessed his star quality. How? You may well ask. He was small, pale, short-sighted, his badly cut hair hanging round his collar and giving him side-whiskers. He puckered up his face as if in the sun. He skipped as he walked. It was as if for him the pavements were made of rubber. He pulled little pages of copybooks out of his pockets, which he screwed into a ball. He smoothed them out with the palm of his hand and, hampered by one of the cigarettes he rolled himself, tried to read a very short poem. He glued it to his eye.

These poems were not like any others of the period I am talking about. Rather they contradicted that period and relied on nothing that came before. Let me say, in passing, that this superb touch, this isolation of words, this density of emptiness, this ventilation of the whole, has so far not been noticed by anyone in France and the many pastiches which they try to sell do not even amount to a caricature.

He gave ancient formulas back their youth. He rubbed down banalities. He cleaned up the commonplace. Whenever he touched them, it was as if his clumsy fingers were putting shells back into water. This was his privilege. He alone could lay claim to it.

'One should be precious,' he would say and in his mouth the word precious gave one a sense of great rarity, as of a precious stone.

We met continually. He idled around. He lived at Parc Saint-Maur with his family, would miss the train, return on foot, walk through the wood and as if he were a child, dread hearing the roar of the lions in the zoo. If he stayed in Paris he slept at some painter's, on a table, among tubes of paint and brushes. He talked little. If he wanted to inspect a canvas or a script, he would take a pair of broken spectacles out of his pocket and use them as an eyeglass.

Not only did he invent and teach us this idea, which was startlingly new, of not appearing original (which he called wearing a new suit); not only did he advise us to write 'like everybody else', because it is just by way of the impossible that originality can express itself, but he also set us the example of work. For that lazy creature (I had to lock him in his room to make him finish a chapter), that bad schoolboy who would escape through the window and scamp his homework (he always went back to it in the end), had become a Chinaman crouching over his books. He used to read masses of mediocre works, comparing them with masterpieces, returning to them, taking notes, annotating, rolling cigarettes and declaring that, since the mechanics of a masterpiece are invisible, he could only learn from books which passed as such but in fact were not.

His rages were rare but terrible. He grew pale as death. Jean Hugo and Georges Auric must remember one evening beside the lake at Arcachon, when we were all reading round a kitchen table. I was tactless enough to say that Moréas wasn't so bad. I read his verses. Radiguet rose, snatched the book from me, crossed the beach, flung it in the water and returned with the face of a murderer, unforgettable.

His novels, specially in my opinion *Le Diable au Corps*, as astonishing in their way as Rimbaud's poems, have never had any help from our modern encyclopaedists. Radiguet was too unorthodox. And it was he who taught me not to lean on anything.

Doubtless he had a plan; he was carrying out a long-term programme. He would, one day, have orchestrated his work, and even, I feel sure, have taken all practical steps to make it known. He was awaiting his moment. Death took him first.

That is why, as I got from him what little perception I possess, his death left me without guidance, incapable of steering my boat, of helping my work and making provision for it.

On my physique

I have never had a beautiful face. Youth stood me in the stead of beauty. My bony structure is good. The flesh hangs badly upon it. Morever in the long run the skeleton changes and gets spoilt. My nose, which used to be straight, is becoming as Roman as my grandfather's. And I noticed that on her death-bed, my mother's too had become Roman. Too many inner storms, sufferings, attacks of doubt, rebellions suppressed by sheer force, cudgellings of fate, have wrinkled my forehead, dug a deep crease between my eyebrows, weighted down my eyelids, slackened my hollow cheeks, turned down the corners of my mouth, in such a way that if I lean over a low mirror I see my mask separating itself from the bone and taking on a shapeless form. My beard sprouts white. My hair, while losing its thickness, has kept its rebellion. This has resulted in a tangle of locks growing in all directions which cannot be combed. If they are smoothed down they give me a seedy look. If they stand on end this hirsute coiffure looks like a sign of affectation.

My teeth overlap. In brief, on a body neither tall nor short, slim and lean, equipped with feet and hands that are admired

because they are long and very expressive, I carry an unreward-
ing head. It gives me a false arrogance. This false arrogance
comes from a desire to conquer the embarrassment I feel at showing myself as I am, and its quickness in disappearing from the
fear that it might be mistaken for real arrogance.

This results in too swift a transition from reserve to effusion,
from self-assurance to awkwardness. Hatred is unknown to me.
I forget injuries so completely that I am apt to smile at my
enemies when I meet them face to face. Their astonishment is
a cold douche and wakes me up. I don't know which way to
look. I am astonished that they remember the wrong they did
to me, which I had forgotten.

It is this natural bent to live in accordance with the Gospels
that draws me away from dogma. Joan of Arc is my great writer.
No one finds truer expression than she does in form or in substance.[1] Without any doubt she would have been blunted had
she adopted a style. As she is, she is style itself, and I never tire
of reading and re-reading the reports of her trial. Antigone is
my other saint. Those two anarchists measure up to the seriousness I like, which Gide denies in my work, my own brand
of seriousness that does not conform to what is usually called
by this name. It is that of the poet. Scholars of every age scorn
it. If it makes them jealous, without them admitting it to themselves, they may go to the length of crime. Voltaire, Diderot,
Grimm only display an attitude as old as the world and one
which will only disappear with me. One that is opposed to poets
and turns against them curved weapons, very terrible at close
range.

Rousseau has left bloody traces of this man-hunt all the way
to Hume where the kill was to take place. Let none believe that
such relentlessness evaporates. Something remains. Rousseau
will always be an instance of persecution mania. He had it. But

[1] Glory through the medium of a minority can only be the prerogative
of artists. This system would not work for politicians, but sometimes pride
induces them to take the risk. Failing unanimity, the majority harms them.
So then they fall back on this minority which, during their term of office,
would not have been strong enough. The case of Joan of Arc is different.
Her ballot is small. She has only three voices. However, they count. Joan
of Arc is a poet.

he was given cause for it. As well blame the stag at bay for using its horns.

On my escapes

I find the source of that fear of the Church, which drives me towards Joan of Arc, in her trial and in *Les Provinciales*. Reading this work has always filled me with consternation, as has the fact that a mind like Pascal's, even if he had to plead the cause of the just, could consent to examine such balderdash.

Several people have dispelled my fear, among them Jacques Maritain and Charles Henrion, for indeed the respect which they inspire brings one's soul to its knees. But the singular quality they have is subordinated to a plurality, to a narrow rule which they make boundless, into which we are dragged by our faith in them, whereupon the bounds appear and imprison us on every hand. It was when I became aware of this manoeuvre, to which they submit without guile, that I took to my heels, as swiftly as I could and ratted. Their heart, my faith, my sincerity remain with me.

La Lettre à Maritain bears witness to this attack of doubt. I thought I could transfer to God's account what was usually credited to the Devil's. In it I set up hardness against purity. I referred to an admirable saying of Maritain's: 'The Devil is pure because he can do nothing but evil.' If purity is not softness asserting itself, but a concrete matter, why should not such matter, rejected by weak goodness, be adopted by hard goodness, and so once more become part of it? I was ingenuous.

In the gentle hands of priests a bomb only explodes if they so wish. They caught mine in mid-air and, wrapping it in layer upon layer of cotton wool, made of it an article of conversion, that is to say an example. My enemies saw in it nothing but a reactionary move. This futile attempt brought me nothing but a family and that outer support which some seek in the family, others in the Church, in sects, in the Ecole Normale, in Polytechnics, in the Foreign Office, in a political party or in a café. Such support upset the habit I had long formed of not leaning on anything but myself.

Maritain found my going heavy. He wanted to open a way for me. It was his own he opened to me. Alas I could not keep up with him, possessing neither the wings of angels nor the vast spiritual mechanism of that soul in the guise of a body. Deprived of my legs, nothing was left to me but fatigue. I escaped.

I was listening last night to a young captain in my hotel telling me about his escapes from Germany and Spain. Back in France, after getting to London via Gibraltar, he suffers from a feeling of flatness and misses adventure. The same problem faces the whole of a younger generation, unconscious of the existence of internal wars, internal prisons, internal escapes, mortal dangers and internal tortures, and so, not knowing what it is to live, only catching a fortuitous glimpse of it and thinking itself no longer alive because circumstances no longer present it with the means to live. Mlle X . . . was a nurse in the American army. Women who do not tend the wounded revolt her. The least comfort shocks her. An elegant woman is an insult to her. She never suspects that this is the maternal instinct working in her, for which, lacking marriage and children, she makes another outlet.

It is in this way that a war is disastrous. If it does not kill, it transmits to some an energy alien to their own resources; to others it permits what the law forbids and accustoms them to short cuts. It artificially glorifies ingenuity, pity, daring. A whole younger generation believes itself to be sublime and collapses when it has to draw on itself for patriotism and fate.

The surprise of these exiles from drama would be great if they were to discover that those tragic episodes, whose sudden cessation has left them on the brink of a void, are just as plentiful in this void as in themselves. That it would be enough to retreat into themselves and pay the costs within instead of without. If the war could enlighten them as to how to use their talents on their own later on, it would be a rough school. But it only gives them an excuse for living faster and real life appears to them like death. When I write that I escaped, after the letter to Maritain, I mean this literally. I experienced all the palpitations, the anguish, the uncertainty, the patience, the resourcefulness about which that captain used to talk to me. And this was not my first escape, nor my last. I have more than one to my credit.

Jacques Maritain often visited me at the clinic where I was disintoxicating myself of opium. I had taken opium, formerly taken daily by our masters under the label of laudanum or opiates, in order to alleviate intolerable nervous pains. After the death of Raymond Radiguet, whom I thought of as my son, these pains had gained such an ascendency that Louis Laloy, at Monte Carlo, advised the palliative. Opium is a living substance. It does not like to be hustled. It made me ill. It was only after a quite long trial that it came to my aid. But it slowed up the works and I feared it. My numerous attempts to flee from it, my checks, my relapses, my success (due to Dr Lichwitz) after five failures, would be worth dwelling on at length. How many cells I escape from, how many sentries take aim at me, how many fortresses I am led back to, the walls of which I succeed in vaulting!

My first important escape (for I do not count those from school, my flight to Marseilles and other escapades) was in 1912. I came of a family that loved music and painting, and for whom literature meant little or nothing. My father used to paint. Whenever an artist opens his box I smell the oil paints. I see him. My grandfather collected excellent pictures, Stradivarius and Greek busts. He arranged quartets. In which he played the cello. I drew. I wrote. I gave myself up, blindly, to gifts, which if they are not channelled, scatter our efforts and act like a pox. Naturally people flattered me. I met no obstacles. I found followers. I succeeded in bewitching a fair number and in being intoxicated with my mistakes.

Without any doubt this line was leading straight to the *Académie*. One day I met Gide. He made me ashamed of my writing. I was embellishing it with arabesques. He was the source of a sudden awakening, the approach to which cost me dear. Few people will allow one to discover oneself. They accuse us of going over to the other camp. Deserter here, suspect there: it is the loneliness of Calchas.[1]

The Russian Ballet of Serge de Diaghilev played its part in this critical phase. He was splashing Paris with colour. The first time I attended one of his performances (they were giving *Le Pavillon d'Armide*) I was in a stall rented by my family. The whole thing unfolded far away behind the footlights, in that burning bush in which the theatre blazes for those who do not regularly go backstage.

I met Serge de Diaghilev at Madame Sert's. From that moment I became a member of the company. I no longer saw Nijinsky except from the wings or from the box in which behind Madame Sert, topped with her Persian aigrette, Diaghilev followed his dancers with a pair of tiny mother-of-pearl opera glasses.

What memories I have of all this! What could I not write about it! That is not my purpose. After the scandal of *Le Sacre*, I went to join Stravinsky at Leysin, where he was looking after his wife. There I finished the *Potomak*, begun at Offranville at J. E. Blanche's house, under the eye of Gide. Returning to Maisons-Laffitte I decided to put an end to it or to be reborn. I became a recluse. I tortured myself. I questioned myself. I insulted myself. I punished myself with self-denial.

I kept nothing of myself but the ashes. The war came. It found me well prepared to escape its traps, to judge what it

[1] The Greek soothsayer. E.S.

brings, what it takes away and how it delivers us from stupidity, now busy elsewhere. I had the good fortune to be living close to the marines. Among them an incredible freedom of thought prevailed. I have described this in the *Discours du Grand Sommeil* and in *Thomas l'Imposteur*.[2]

I repeat that, in Paris, the field was free. We occupied it. As early as 1916 our revolution began.

After Stravinsky, Picasso. At last I knew the secret without knowledge of which all mental effort is fruitless. A world existed in which the artist finds before he seeks and finds unceasingly. A world where the wars are the wars of religion. Picasso, Stravinsky were its leaders.

One attaches too much importance to the word genius. One is too economical with it. Stendhal used it to describe a woman who knew how to step into a carriage. In this sense I had genius and very little talent. My mind went by instinct straight to the mark, but did not know how to use it. One can guess what the friendship meant to me of the creators of *Les Demoiselles d'Avignon* and of *Les Noces*. I elbowed my way through a mass of quarrels, disputes, trials for heresy. I searched for myself. I thought I recognized myself, I lost sight of myself, I ran after myself, I caught myself up, out of breath. As soon as I succumbed to some spell I was up in arms against it.

That youth progresses by injustice, is justice. For soon enough comes the age of looking back. One returns and can then enjoy what one strode over or trampled underfoot on one's way.

The first chimes of a period which began in 1912 and will only end with my death, were rung for me by Diaghilev, one night in the Place de la Concorde. We were going home, having had supper after the show. Nijinsky was sulking as usual. He was walking ahead of us. Diaghilev was scoffing at my absurdities. When I questioned him about his moderation (I was used to praise), he stopped, adjusted his eyeglass and said: 'Astonish me.' The idea of surprise, so enchanting in Apollinaire, had never occurred to me.

In 1917, the evening of the first performance of *Parade*, I did astonish him.

2 *The Impostor,* translated by Dorothy Williams. Peter Owen 1957. E.S.

This very brave man listened, white as a sheet, to the fury of the house. He was frightened. He had reason to be. Picasso, Satie and I were unable to get back to the wings. The crowd recognized and threatened us. Without Apollinaire, his uniform and the bandage round his head, women armed with pins would have put out our eyes.

A little while later the *Joseph* of Hofmannsthal was given a triumphant reception. I was in his box. At the tenth curtain call Hofmannsthal leant over to Diaghilev: 'I would have preferred a scandal,' he told him. And Diaghilev, in the same manner he had used when he said to me 'Astonish me,' replied to him : 'But you see . . . you see that's not so easy.'

From 1917, when he was fourteen, Raymond Radiguet taught me to distrust the new if it had a new look, to run counter to the fashions of the *avant-garde*. This puts one in an awkward position. One shocks the right. One shocks the left. But, at a distance, all these contradictions come together under one label. Clever the one who can sort this out. The young people who visit our ruins see only one style. The age called 'heroic' displays nothing but its daring. This is how a Museum works. It levels. Ingres and Delacroix side by side, Matisse with Picasso, Braque with Bonnard. And even, let me say, in a recent revival of *Faust*, the old garden set, the work of Jusseaume, had become, thanks to dust and unconscious similarities, a magnificent Claude Monet.

But this phenomenon of perspective does not concern youth. Youth can only assert itself through the conviction that its ventures surpass all others and resemble nothing.

On France

France is a country that disparages herself. This is all to the good, for otherwise she would be the most pretentious country in the world. The essential thing is that she is not self-conscious. Whatever is self-conscious neutralizes itself. In my novel *Les Enfants Terribles* I took great care to show that this sister and this brother were not self-conscious. Had they been conscious of their poetic strength they would at once have been aesthetes and have moved from the active to the passive. No. They loathe themselves. They loathe their room. They want another life. That, no doubt, of such as imitate them and lose their privileges for a world that only exists through the certainty that privileges are elsewhere and that they don't possess any.

I have at home a letter of de Musset's written at the period most rich in genius. He complains that there is not one artist, not one book, not one painter, not one play. The Comédie-Française he says, is crumbling in the dust and Madame Malibran is singing in London because the Opéra sings out of tune. Every period in France has this peculiarity that, with all the richness under her nose, she sees nothing there and looks for it elsewhere.

How ridiculous are those who try to express her greatness in words! 'Greatness, purity, constructive works.' Such is the modern refrain. Meanwhile greatness, purity, constructive works are produced in a form that remains invisible to them and would seem to them a disgrace to the country. And the critics judge the works and do not realize that they are judged by them. Who makes the greatness of France? It is Villon, it is Rimbaud, it is Verlaine, it is Baudelaire. All that splendid company was put in the lock-up. People wanted to drive it out of France. It was left to die in the poorhouse. I do not mean Joan of Arc. With her it's the trial that counts. Sad is her revenge. Poor Péguy! I was so fond of him. He was an anarchist. What would he say of the use made of his name?

France's attitude after the liberation was simple. She did not take one. Under the yoke of armed force, how could she? What line should she have taken? Said to the world: 'I didn't want to fight. I don't like to fight. I had no weapons. I shall not have any. I possess a secret weapon. What? Since it is secret, how can I answer you?' And if the world insists: *'My secret weapon is a tradition of anarchy.'*

That is a powerful answer. An enigma. Enough to perplex the great powers. 'Invade me. All the same in the long run I shall possess you.'

Since such a Chinese attitude has not been adopted and we have talked a lot of hot air, what chance is now left to us? To become a village, as Lao-Tze advocates. To be no longer enviable save through the invisible, more spacious than the visible, and sovereign.

Lao-Tze, speaking of the ideal empire, says: 'To hear the cocks from one end of the land to the other.'

What is France, I ask you? A cock on a dung-heap. Remove the dung, the cock dies. That's what happens when you push folly to the point of confusing a dung-heap with a heap of garbage.

On the theatre

Ever since as a child I watched my mother and my father leaving for the theatre, I have suffered from the fever of crimson and gold. I never get used to it. Every curtain that rises takes me back to that solemn moment when, as the curtain of the Châtelet rose on *Round the World in Eighty Days*, the chasms of darkness and of light became one, separated by the footlights. These footlights set the bottom of the wall of painted canvas aglow. As this flimsy wall did not touch the boards, one obtained a glimpse of coming and going in a furnace. Apart from this gap the only aperture by which the two worlds communicated was a hole edged with brass. The smell of the circus was one thing. The narrow box with its uncomfortable little chairs was another. And as in the rooms of Mena-House, where the windows open on to the Pyramids, in the little box the oceanic murmur of the audience hits you in the face, the cry of the attendants: 'Peppermints, caramels, acid-drops,' the crimson cavern and the chandelier which Baudelaire liked better than the show.

As time passes, the theatre I work in does not lose its prestige.

I respect it. It overawes me. It fascinates me. There I divide
in two. I live in it and I become the child permitted by the
ticket seller to enter Hades.

When I put on *La Voix Humaine* at the Comédie-Française,
and later *Renaud et Armide*, I was astonished that my colleagues should consider this theatre to be the same as any other
and would produce plays there written for no matter where.
The Comédie-Française remained in my eyes that house of
marble and velvet haunted by the great shades of my youth.
Yesterday, Maraist telephoned from Paris saying they had asked
him to return there, but this time on first-class terms. He
asked my advice, no doubt in order that I might dissuade
him. I have a number of reasons for doing so. But I hesitated
to reply. The naïve respect which this theatre rouses in me
had just waved its red cape. In a flash I saw Mounet-Sully
crossing the stage from right to left in the guise of the young
Ruy Blas. He was old. His beard was white. Almost blind, his
head sunken between his shoulders, he held a candelabrum.
And his walk was the Spaniard's.

I saw de Max, with a hand covered in rings, shaking his
black locks in the air and trailing his veils. I saw Madame
Bartet, old bird without a neck, singing Andromache. I saw
Madame Segond-Weber, in *Rodogune*, poisoned, and goose-
stepping off the stage with her tongue out.

All this was hardly likely to encourage a young man. And
yet I hesitated to say to him : 'refuse'. Once the receiver was
hung up again, those superb old-stagers were still operative.
Reason told me : 'This actor has just made your film. He is
acting in your play. He is to act in your next. He is in demand
everywhere. He is highly paid. He is free.' Unreason showed
me the child that I had been, led to my Thursday seat by
an attendant with a pink bow and a grey moustache, and
Marais in that frame of gold, playing the part of Nero in
which he is incomparable.

That's how I am, ensnared by charms. Swiftly dazzled. I
belong to the moment. It falsifies my perspective. It puts a
stopper on diversity. I give way to anyone who knows how to
get round me. I take on responsibilities. I dawdle over them

and miss the mark right and left. That is why solitude is good for me. It reunites my quicksilver.

The sun which had been shining is veiled in mist. The motley families depart. The hotel empties and I can do my holiday tasks. Between two pages of writing I search for the title of my play. Now that it is finished the title eludes me. And the title *La Reine Morte*, which would suit it, troubles me greatly. My queen has no name. The pseudonym of Stanislas: Azraël, is suitable, but they tell me that this would be remembered as Israël. One title alone exists. It will be, so it is. Time conceals it from me. How discover it, covered by a hundred others? I have to avoid *the* this, *the* that. Avoid the image. Avoid the descriptive and the undescriptive. Avoid the exact meaning and the inexact. The soft, the hard. Neither long nor short. Right to catch the eye, the ear, the mind. Simple to read and to remember. I had announced several. I had to repeat them twice and the journalists still got them wrong. My real title defies me. It enjoys its hiding-place, like a child one keeps calling, and whom one believes drowned in the pond.[1]

The theatre is a furnace. Whoever does not suspect this is consumed in the long run or else burns out at once. It damps one's zeal. It attacks by fire and by water.

The audience is a surging sea. It gives one nausea. This is called stage fright. It's all very well to say to oneself: it's the theatre, it's the audience. It makes no difference. One makes up one's mind not to be caught again. One returns. It's the Casino. One stakes all one has. It's exquisite torture. Anyone but a conceited ass goes through it. There is no cure.

When I rehearse I become a spectator. I am bad at correcting faults. I love actors and they take me in. I listen to something other than myself. The night before the show my weaknesses stare me in the face. It is too late. Consequently, overcome by something very like sea-sickness, I stride up and down the ship, the bunkers, the cabins, the alleyways to the

[1] This was *L'Aigle à Deux Têtes* (*The Eagle with Two Heads*).

cabins. I dare not look at the sea. Still less dip into it. It seems
to me that if I were to enter the auditorium I would sink the
ship.

Here am I then in the wings, straining my ears. Behind
the set a play is no longer painted; it draws its own outline.
It shows me its flaws in draughtsmanship. I go out. I go and
lie down in the dressing-rooms. What my actresses leave there,
when changing souls, creates an inevitable vacuum. I suffocate.
I get up. I listen. Where have they got to? I listen at doors.
Yet I know this sea is subject to rules. Its waves roll in and roll
out at my command. A new house reacts to the same effects.
But let one of those effects be unduly prolonged and the actor
falls into the trap. With difficulty he refuses the rescuing hand
of laughter. Such cruel laughter should wound him; it flatters
him. 'I suffer and I make them laugh,' he tells himself, 'at this
game I win.' The rescuing hand is quickly offered and quickly
grasped, the author forgotten. The boat drifts and you will soon
be wrecked. If the actors listen to these sirens, the drama
becomes melodrama, the thread connecting the scenes is broken.
The rhythm is lost.

From afar I supervise my crew badly. The 'imponderables'
escape me. What am I to change? Here are the interpreters
who check over and perfect the machine. Here are those who
live on the stage and try to conquer the machinery. Diderot
speaks lightly. He was not born on the boards.

I know authors who supervise the actors and write them
notes. They achieve discipline. They paralyse. They lock the
door that might have suddenly blown open.

Two great schools of acting confront each other on the stage.
They, the authors, prevent the one from embellishing its straight
line with some inspired invention, they wake the other from its
hypnosis. I prefer to risk the chemistry. Either red or black will
come up.

Writing this paragraph I seem to be in the dressing-room
of my actor, Marcel André, with whom I like to discuss such
things. Yvonne de Bray and Jean Marais are on the stage.
Their temperaments harmonize. One wonders by what mechanism they respect the dialogue they are living, forgetting that

one wall of the room they are in is missing. Marcel André is
speaking. I listen to him. I also listen to the silence of the
house. He, for his part, is listening for the call-bell that will
bring him into the play. We are only half alive.

Delicious moments of suffering that I would not exchange
for anything.

Why do you write plays? I am asked by the novelist. Why
do you write novels? I am asked by the dramatist. Why do you
make films? I am asked by the poet. Why do you draw? I am
asked by the critic. Why do you write? I am asked by the
draughtsman? Yes, why? I wonder. Doubtless so that my
seed may be blown all over the place. I know little about this
breath within me, but it is not gentle. It cares not a jot for the
sick. It is unmoved by fatigue. It takes advantage of my gifts.
It wants to do its part. It is not inspiration, it's expiration one
should say. For this breath comes from a zone in man into
which man cannot descend, even if Virgil were to lead him there,
for Virgil himself did not descend into it.

What have I to do with genius? It only seeks an accomplice
in me. What it wants is an excuse to succeed in its evil deeds.

The main thing, if our action is divided, is not to fuse our
efforts. I never settle for one of its branches without amputating
others. I prune myself. It is even pretty rare for me to draw
in the margins of a piece of writing. That is why I have published albums of drawings relating to my writings but not together. If I did publish them together, the drawings were made
a long time afterwards. In *Portraits-Souvenir* I drew on the
spot. The articles appeared in *Le Figaro* and articles and
drawings of that kind can be done with the same ink.

Still less could I direct theatre and cinema as a team, for
they turn their backs on one another. While I was making my
film *La Belle et la Bête*, the Gymnase was rehearsing my play
Les Parents Terribles. The cast accused me of being inattentive.
Even though I was no longer actually filming, I was the slave
of a task in which the language is visual and is not crammed
into a frame. I own I had the greatest trouble on earth in

listening to an immobile text and giving it all my attention. Once a work is completed, I have to wait before undertaking another. The completed work does not release me quickly. It moves its chattels slowly. The wise thing then is a change of air and of room. The new material comes to me on my walks. Whatever happens I mustn't notice it. If I interfere, it doesn't come any more. One fine day the work demands my help. I give myself up to it in one fell swoop. My pauses are its own. If it falls asleep my pen skids. As soon as it wakes, it gives me a shake. It couldn't care less if I am asleep. Get up, it says, so that I can dictate. And it is not easy to follow. Its vocabulary is not of words.

In *Opium* I describe a liberty I took during *Les Enfants Terribles*. Seduced by the flow of my pen, I believed I was free to invent for myself. Everything stood still. I had to await its *good pleasure*.

La Machine Infernale used another mood. It would desert me for very long periods. It would wait for other fevers to cease distracting me. It wanted me for itself. If my mind wandered at all, it turned its back on me. *La Machine à Ecrire* is a disaster. From the first, when I thought myself ready to write it, another inspiration took over and dictated *La Fin du Potomak*. I wanted to return to it. I took the dictation badly. After the first act I just wrote it my own way. Once the play was written, I persistently rewrote it. And after all that I listened to advice and ruined the end. May that play be an example to me! I shall never be my own master. I am made for obedience. And these lines that I am writing, a week ago I did not know I had to write.

Of all the problems that confuse us, that of fate and of free will is the most obscure. What? The thing is written in advance and we can write it, we can change the end? The truth is different. Time does not exist. It is what enfolds us. What we believe we carry out later is done all in one piece. Time reels it off for us. Our work is already done. However we still have to discover it. It is this passive participation which is so astounding. And with reason. It leaves the public incredulous. I decide and I do not decide. I obey and I direct. It's a great mystery.

La Machine à Ecrire was not a bad play to begin with.[2] The juice left me high and dry. I was free. But I am no longer free to remove the blot I made. It is there.

---

[2] This play is now included in the repertoire of the Comédie Française in a new version.

On Diaghilev and Nijinsky

In a book in which I bear witness to the Socratic proceedings that society institutes against us, I must express my gratitude to two free men who lived to cry their cries.

Nijinsky was of less than average height. In soul and in body he was just a professional deformity.

His face, of Mongol type, was joined to his body by a very long and very thick neck. The muscles of his thighs and those of his calves stretched the fabric of his trousers and gave him the appearance of having legs bent backwards. His fingers were short, as if cut off at the knuckles. In short, one would never have believed that this little monkey with sparse hair, wearing a skirted overcoat and a hat balanced on the top of his head, was the idol of the public.

Yet he was, and with good reason. Everything about him was designed to be seen at a distance, in the limelight. On the stage his over-developed muscles became slim. His figure lengthened (his heels never touching the ground), his hands became the fluttering leaves of his gestures, and as for his face, it was radiant.

Such a metamorphosis is almost unimaginable for those who never witnessed it.

In *Le Spectre de la Rose*, in which he epitomized himself from 1913 onwards he performed with a bad grace. Because the choreography of *Le Sacre* shocked people, and he could not bear it that the one should be applauded and the other booed. Gravity is a part of our being. He tried endlessly to find some trick to get the better of it.

He had become aware that half of the leap which ends *Le Spectre de la Rose* was lost when seen from the auditorium. He invented a double leap, twisting himself in mid-air and falling vertically into the wings. There they received him like a prize fighter, with hot towels, slaps, and water which his servant Dimitri spat in his face.

Before the opening of *Le Faune*, at supper at Larue's, he astonished us for several days by moving his head as if he had a stiff neck. Diaghilev and Bakst were anxious, questioned him and got no answer. We learned later that he had been training himself to stand the weight of the horns. I could quote a thousand instances of this perpetual rehearsing which made him sullen and moody.

At the Hôtel Crillon (Diaghilev and he used to migrate from hotel to hotel, chased by fear of having their belongings distrained), he would put on a bath wrap, pull the hood over his head and make notes for his choreographies.

I saw him create all his roles. His deaths were poignant. That of *Pétrouchka*, in which the puppet becomes human enough to move us to tears. That of *Schéhérazade* in which he drummed the boards like a fish in the bottom of a boat.

Serge de Diaghilev appeared to wear the smallest hat in the world. If you put this hat on, it came right down to your ears. For his head was so large that any head-covering was too small for him.

His dancers nicknamed him *Chinchilla* because of one lock kept white in his dyed and very black hair. He stuffed himself into a coat with a collar of opossum, and sometimes fastened it with the help of safety-pins. His face was that of a mastiff, his smile that of a very young crocodile, one tooth sticking over his lip. Sucking at his teeth was with him a sign of pleasure, of fear, of anger. He chewed his lips, topped by a little moustache, in the back of some stage-box from which he kept an eye on his artists in whom he let nothing pass. And his watery eye was cast down with the curve of a Portuguese oyster. This man led across the globe a company of dancers as confused and motley as the fair at Nijni-Novgorod. The only luxury for him was to discover a star. And we saw him bring us out of the Russian ghetto the thin, long, glaucous Madame Rubinstein. She did not dance. She entered, she showed herself, she mimed, she walked, she went out, and sometimes (as in *Schéhérazade*) she ventured on a sketch of a dance.

One of Diaghilev's triumphs was to present her to Paris audiences in the role of Cleopatra. That is to say to present her to Antony. A bale of material was brought on. It was set in the middle of the stage. It was unrolled, unpacked. And Madame Ida Rubinstein appeared, so thin-legged that you thought you were seeing an ibis from the Nile.

I am drawing these figures in the margin of the programmes of great occasions that played a decisive part in my love of the theatre. Indeed a reference to Vestris, to Talma whets my appetite. I should like to read more about them.

On the marvels of cinematography

The word marvellous is in constant use. But we need to agree on its meaning none the less. If I had to define it, I should say that it is what removes us from the confines within which we have to live, and is like a 'fatigue' which is drawn outwards at our birth and at our death.

There is a fallacy that gives rise to the belief that the cinematograph is a suitable art to bring this faculty of the spirit into play. This fallacy is due to a hasty confusion of marvels with conjuring tricks. It is no great marvel to produce a dove from a hat. The proof is that this sort of trick can be bought, can be taught, and that such miracles at two a penny follow fashion. They are no more marvellous than is algebra, but present a frivolous and pleasing appearance, less of a strain on the intelligence. Does this mean that the cinematograph cannot put in our hands a weapon able to out-distance the target? No. But if it can do so, it is on the same basis as the other arts, from which people try to exclude it because its youth makes it suspect in a country (France) where, except when it is a matter of defending the soil, youth is not taken into consideration.

The cinematograph is fifty years old. My own age, alas. A lot for me. Very little for a Muse who expresses herself through the medium of ghosts and with equipment still in its infancy if one compares it with the use of paper and ink.

It seems likely that the remark 'Do write about the marvels of the cinematograph,' derives from the films *Le Sang d'un Poète* and *La Belle et la Bête*, conceived at an interval of fifteen years, and in which everyone sees the embodiment of that curiosity which impels us to open forbidden doors, to walk in the dark humming to keep up our courage.

Now, *Le Sang d'un Poète* is only a descent into oneself, a way of using the mechanism of the dream without sleeping, a crooked candle, often mysteriously blown out, carried about in the night of the human body. There the actions link as they please, under so feeble a control that one could not ascribe it to the mind. Rather to a kind of somnolence helping memories to break out, free to combine, to entwine, to distort themselves until they take shape unknown to us and become for us an enigma.

Nowhere is less fitted than France for the exercise of this faculty which has recourse neither to reason nor to symbols. Few French people are prepared to enjoy an exceptional event without knowing its source, its object, or without investigating it. They prefer to laugh at it and treat it with contempt.

The symbol is their last resort. It gives them some scope. It also allows them to explain the incomprehensible and to endow with hidden meaning whatever draws its beauty from not having any. 'Why? Is it a joke? Whose leg are you pulling?' are the weapons that France uses against the new form, which some proud spirit takes on when it manifests itself, contrary to all expectation, and intrigues a few of the open-minded.

These few open-minded people are at once taken to be accomplices. Sometimes snobs, who have inherited the flair of kings, follow them blindly. This creates a mix-up which the general public cold-shoulders, incapable of recognizing the signs of a new embryonic form which it will acclaim tomorrow. And so forth. The marvellous then, since a prodigy can only be a prodigy in so far as a natural phenomenon still eludes us, would be not the miracle that sickens by the disorder it causes, but the simple miracle, human and absolutely down to earth, which consists in giving to objects and to people an unusual quality that defies analysis. As is proved to us by Vermeer of Delft.

This painter certainly paints what he sees, but such accuracy, pleasing to everyone, shows us where he deviates from it. For if he does not use any artifice to surprise us, our surprise is the more profound, faced with the peculiarities which earn him his uniqueness and preclude us from making the slightest comparison between his work and that of his contemporaries. Any other painter of the same school paints with the same frankness. It is a pity that such frankness does not divulge any secret for us. In Vermeer space is peopled from another world than the one he depicts. The subject of his picture is only a pretext, a vehicle through which to express the realm of the marvellous.

This is what I was coming to: that the cinematograph can ally itself with the marvellous, as I see it, if it is content to be a vehicle for it and if it does not try to produce it. The kind of rapture that transports us when in contact with certain works is seldom due to any attempt to move us to tears, or to any surprise effect. It is rather, I repeat, induced in an inexplicable manner by a breach which opens unawares.

This breach will occur in a film in the same way as in a tragedy, a novel or a poem. The rapture will not come from its opportunities for trickery. It will come from some error, from some syncope, from some chance encounter between the attention and inattention of its author.[1] Why should he behave differently from the Muses? His talent for deceiving the eye and the mind also deceives one about his claim to nobility.

Cinematography is an art. It will free itself from the industrial bondage whose platitudes no more condemn it than bad pictures and bad books discredit painting and literature.

But, for mercy's sake, don't go taking it for a magician. This is the way people talk about a craftsman, avoiding by this

[1] And the capacity for wonder of the spectator. You get nothing for nothing.

term fathoming his ventures. His gift does not lie in card tricks. He goes beyond jugglery. That is only his syntax. It is elsewhere that we must salute the marvellous. *Le Sang d'un Poète* contains no magic, nor does *La Belle et la Bête*.

The characters in the latter film obey the rule of fairy-tales. Nothing surprises them in a world where things are accepted as normal, the least of which would disrupt the mechanism of ours. When Beauty's necklace changes into a piece of old rope, it is not this phenomenon that shocks her sisters, but the fact that it changes into rope because they touch it.

And if the marvellous is to be found in my film, it is not in this direction that one should expect it; it will show rather in the eyes of the Beast when he says to Beauty: 'You caress me as one caresses an animal', and she answers him: 'But you are an animal.'

Indolence, in the robes of a judge, condemns, in our poetic ventures, what it considers unpoetic, basing its verdict upon that semblance of the marvellous of which I am speaking, and deaf to the marvellous if it does not bear its attributes.

When one sees fairies they disappear. They only help us in a guise which makes them unrecognizable and are only present through the sudden unwonted grace of familiar objects into which they disguise themselves in order to keep us company. It is then that their help becomes effective and not when they appear and dazzle us with lights. It is the same with everything. In *La Belle et la Bête* I have not made use of that slope down which the public would like to slide more and more rapidly without it being spared any dizziness.

I persist in repeating: Marvels and Poetry are not my affair. They must ambush me. My itinerary must not foresee them. If I opine that a certain shady place is more favourable than another to shelter them, I am cheating. For it may happen that a road exposed to full sunlight shelters them better.

This is why I care to live just as much in Beauty's family as in the Beast's castle. This is why fairy-like atmosphere means more to me than the fairy element itself. This is why the episode, among others, of the sedan chairs in the farmyard, an episode which does not spring from any fantasy, is, in my opinion, more significant of this fairy quality than any artifice of the castle.

In *Le Sang d'un Poète*, the blood that flows throughout the film disturbs our critics. What is the point, they ask, of disgusting and shocking us on purpose? This blood which sickens us compels us to turn our heads away and prevents us from enjoying the happy inventions (by happy inventions they mean: the entry into the mirror, the statue that moves, the heart that beats), but from one to another of these shocks that awaken them what link is there, I ask you, except this blood which flows and from which the film derives its title? What do they know of the great river, those who only want to enjoy the ports of call? And what would these happy inventions, as they call them, be worth, if they were not the result of an architecture, even if an unconscious one, and connected to the rest by this bond of blood? They sleep and think that I sleep and that my awakening wakens them. Their torpor condemns them to taste nothing of a meal but the pepper. They feel nothing but the pricks. It is these that excite them, give them the fidgets, compel them to run from place to place.

In *l'Eternel Retour* the lovers' castle seems to them right for poetry. The brother's and sister's garage wrong. They condemn it. Strange foolishness. Because it is precisely in this garage that poetry functions best. In fact to understand the surrender of the brother and sister to their innate and, as it were, organic disregard of grace, poetry is at our finger-tips – and I draw closer to the terrible mysteries of love.

Such is the fruit of certain experiments I have made, which I am still carrying out, and which are the sole object of my quest.

As Montaigne says: 'Most of Aesop's fables have several meanings and interpretations. Those who make myths of them choose some aspect that accords well with the fable; but for the most part this is only the first superficial aspect, and there are others more vital, more essential and innate, which they have been unable to penetrate.'

On friendship

The Prince de Polignac used to say: 'I don't really like other people.' But when his wife asks him: 'Why are you so gloomy?' and he replies: 'I like some people and some people like me,' and adds: 'Alas! They are not the same people,' he admits his loneliness. I like other people and only exist through them. Without them the balls I serve go into the net. Without them my flame burns low. Without them my flame sinks. Without them I am a ghost. If I withdraw from my friends I seek their shadows.

Sometimes stupidity and lack of culture take their place. I am taken in by the slightest kindness. But then, how am I to make myself understood? They do not know what I am talking about. So therefore I must find a means of being understood. Do I go too fast? Is it due to syncopation? Are the letters of my words not large enough? I search. I find. I speak. They listen to me. And this is not the need for exercise. It is the taste for human contact.

I have said somewhere that I am better at making friends

than at making love. Love is mainly an affair of short spasms.
If these spasms disappoint us, love dies. It is very seldom that
it weathers the experience and becomes friendship. Friendship
between man and woman is delicate; it is still a form of love.
In it jealousy is disguised. Friendship is a quiet spasm. Without possessiveness. The happiness of a friend delights us. It adds
to us. It takes nothing away. If friendship takes offence at this,
it does not exist. It is a love that conceals itself. I strongly suspect that this passion for friendship that I have always had
comes to me from the sons of whom I am cheated. As I cannot
have them I invent them. I should like to educate them. But
I perceive that it is they who educate me. Apart from the fact
that youth, and its presence in our house, compels us never to
take any step which could not set it an example, it has weapons
suited to its struggles for which ours are out of date. We have
to learn from it. It has little to learn from us. Later our essence
impregnates it and makes for it a soil in which to bloom.
Words are futile. In my school one would hear the flight of
a fly. And I'm a chatterbox.

The giving of guidance if asked for is quite another thing.
I don't excel in that either. I talk fluently about something
else and it is by this means that I am of service.

Max Jacob used to say to me: 'You have no sense of companionship.' He was right. What Wilde said to Pierre Louys
suits me better. Failing to understand him, he made a scandal
of it: 'I have no friends. I have only lovers.' A dangerous
construction if it comes to the ears of the police or a man of
letters. He meant to say that he always went to extremes. I
think in this he was simply putting on side. He might have
said: 'I only have companions.' And if I had been Pierre
Louys, I should have been still more offended.

Where would I find pleasure in companionship? When
I trail from café to café, from studio to studio, arm in arm
with companions? Friendship occupies all my time and if any
work distracts me from it, I dedicate this to it. It (friendship)
saves me from that anguish men experience as they grow old.

Youth is not what my friends want of me and theirs only
interests me in so far as it reflects their shadow. Each one uses

it to his advantage, enjoys his fun where he finds it. Tries to remain worthy of the other. And time flies.

'*Our attempt at culture came to a sad end*,' said Verlaine. Alas how many failures I record! There was reason enough for flight. But the soul is tenacious. Destroy its niche, it rebuilds it.

Garros's plane is on fire. It crashes. Jean le Roy arranges my letters fan-shape on his mess-tin. He grasps his machine-gun. He dies. Typhoid carries off Radiguet. Marcel Khill is killed in Alsace. The Gestapo tortures Jean Desbordes.

I know quite well that I used to seek the friendship of machines that spin too fast and wear themselves out dramatically. Today paternal instinct keeps me away from them. I turn towards those who are not marked with the evil star. Cursed be it! I detest it. Once again I warm my carcase in the sunshine.

On dreams

A session at Dr B's, with nitrogen protoxyde comes to my mind. The nurse is giving this to me. The door opens. Another nurse comes in and says the word *Madame*. I leave our world, not without believing that I am countering the gas with a superior lucidity. I even seem to have the strength to make some very subtle remarks. 'Doctor, take care, I am not asleep.' But the journey begins. It lasts for centuries. I reach the first tribunal. I am judged. I pass. Another century. I reach the second tribunal. I am judged. I pass and so it continues. At the fourteenth tribunal I understand that multiplicity is the sign of this other world and unity the sign of ours. I shall find on return one body, one dentist, one dentist's room, one dentist's hand, one dentist's lamp, one dentist's chair, one dentist's white coat. And soon I must forget what I have seen. Retrace my steps before all these tribunals. Realize that they know that it is of no importance, that I shall not talk about it because I shall not remember. Centuries are added to centuries. I re-enter our world. I see unity reforming. What a bore! Everything is one. And I hear a voice saying at the door: '. . . wishes to know if you will see her tomorrow.' The nurse is finishing her sentence. Only the name of the lady has escaped me. This is the duration of the centuries from which I'm surfacing, this the expanse of my dizzy journey. It is the immediacy of the dream. All we remember is the interminable dream that occurs instantaneously on the brink of awakening. I have said that my dreams were usually of the nature of caricatures. They accuse me. They inform me of what is irreparable in my nature. They underline organic imperfections I will not correct. I suspected these. The dream proves them to me by means of acts, apologues, speeches. It is not like this every time, unless I flatter myself, not having unravelled the meaning.

The swiftness of the dream is such that its scenes are peopled with objects unknown to us when awake and about which in a trice we know the minutest details. What strikes me is that, from one second to the next, our ego of the dream finds itself projected into a new world, without feeling the astonishment which this world would rouse in it in a waking state, although it remains itself and does not participate in this transfiguration. We ourselves remain in another universe, which might suggest that when falling asleep we are like a traveller who awakes with a start. Nothing of the kind, since the town, where he did not believe himself to be, surprises this traveller, whereas the extravaganzas of a dream never disconcert the waking man who falls asleep. So the dream is the sleeper's normal existence. This is why I endeavour to forget my dreams on waking. The actions of a dream are not valid in a waking state and the actions of the waking state are only valid in the dream because it has the digestive faculty of making them into excrement. In the world of sleep this excrement does not appear to us as such and its chemistry interests us, amuses us or terrifies us. But transposed into the waking state, which does not possess this digestive faculty, the actions of the dream would foul life for us and make it unbreathable. Thousands of examples prove this, because in recent times a good many doors have been opened to these horrors. It is one thing to look for signs in them and another to allow the oil stain to spread over to the waking

state and extend there. Fortunately our neighbour's dream
bores us if he recounts it to us and this fact stops us from re-
counting our own.

What is certain is that this enfolding, through the medium
of which eternity becomes liveable to us, is not produced in
dreams in the same way as in life. Something of this fold unfolds. Thanks to this our limits change, widen. The past, the
future no longer exist; the dead rise again; places construct
themselves without architect, without journeys, without that tedious oppression that compels us to live minute by minute that which
the half-opened fold shows us at a glance. Moreover the atmos-
pheric and profound triviality of the dream favours encounters,
surprises, acquaintanceships, a naturalness, which our enfolded
world (I mean projected on to the surface of a fold) can only
ascribe to the supernatural. I say naturalness, because one of
the characteristics of the dream is that nothing in it astonishes
us. We consent without regret to live there among strangers,
entirely separated from our habits and our friends. This is what
fills us with dismay at the sight of a face we love, and which
is asleep. Where, at this moment, stirs the face behind this mask?
Where does it light up and for whom? This sight of sleep has
always frightened me more than dreams. I made the verses of
Plain-Chant about it.

A woman sleeps. She triumphs. She need no longer lie.
She is a lie from head to toe. She will give no account of her
movements. She deceives with impunity. Taking advantage of
this licentiousness, she parts her lips, she allows her limbs to
drift where they will. She is no longer on guard. She is her own
alibi. What could the man watching her blame her for? She
is there. What need has Othello of that handkerchief? Let him
watch Desdemona sleeping. It is enough to make one commit
murder. It is true that a jealous man never ceases to be one
and that afterwards he would exclaim : 'What is she doing to
me there among the dead?'

Emerged from sleep the dream fades. It is a deep sea plant
which dies out of water. It dies on my sheets. Its reign mystifies
me. I admire its fables. I take advantage of it to live a double life.
I never make use of it.

What it teaches us is the bitterness of our limitations. Since Nerval, Ducasse, Rimbaud, the study of its mechanism has often given the poet the means of conquering them, adapting our world otherwise than according to the dictates of good sense, shuffling the order of the factors to which reason condemns us, in short making for poetry a lighter, swifter and newer vehicle.

On reading

I cannot read or write. And when the census form asks me this question, I am tempted to answer no.

Who knows how to write? It is to battle with ink to try to make oneself understood.

Either one takes too much care over one's work or one does not take enough. Seldom does one find the happy mean that limps with grace. Reading is another matter. I read. I think I am reading. Each time I re-read, I perceive that I have not read. That is the trouble with a letter. One finds in it what one looks for. One is satisfied. One puts it aside. If one finds it again, on re-reading one reads into it another which one had not read.

Books play us the same trick. If they do not suit our present mood we do not consider them good. If they disturb us we criticize them and this criticism is superimposed upon them and prevents us from reading them fairly.

What the reader wants is to read himself. When he reads what he approves of he thinks he could have written it. He may even have a grudge against the book for taking his place, for

saying what he did not know how to say, and which according
to him he would have said better.

The more a book means to us the less well we read it. Our
substance slips into it and thinks it round to our own outlook.
That is why if I want to read and convince myself that I can
read, I read books into which my substance does not penetrate.
In the hospitals in which I spent long periods, I used to read
what the nurse brought me or what fell into my hands by chance.
These were the books of Paul Féval, of Maurice Leblanc, of
Xavier Leroux, and the innumerable adventure books and
detective stories which made of me a modest and attentive reader.
*Rocambole, M. Lecoq, le crime d'Orcival, Fantômes, Chéri-
Bibi*, while saying to me : 'You can read', spoke to me too much
in my own language for me not to get something, unconsciously,
from them, for my mind not to distort them to its own dimen-
sions. This is so true that, for instance, you often hear a
tubercular patient say of Thomas Mann's book *The Magic
Mountain* : 'That is a book one couldn't understand if one
hadn't been tubercular.' In fact Thomas Mann wrote it without
being this and for the very purpose of making those who had not
experienced tuberculosis understand it.

We are all ill and only know how to read books which deal
with our malady. This is why books dealing with love are so
successful, since everyone believes that he is the only one to experience it. He thinks : 'This book is addressed to me. What can
anyone else see in it?' 'How beautiful this book is,' says the one
they love, by whom they believe themselves to be loved and
whom they hasten to make read it. But that person says
this because he or she loves elsewhere.

It is enough to make one wonder if the function of books, all
of which speak to convince, is not to listen and to nod assent.
In Balzac the reader is in his element : 'This is my uncle,' he
tells himself, 'this is my aunt, this is my grandfather, this is
Madame X . . ., this is the town where I was born.' In Dostoiev-
sky what does he tell himself? 'This is my fever and my violence,
of which those around me have no suspicion.'

And the reader believes he is reading. The glass without quicksilver seems to him a true mirror. He recognizes the scene enacted

behind it. How closely it resembles what he is thinking! How
clearly it reflects his image! How well they collaborate, he and
it! How well they *reflect*!

Just as in museums there are certain pictures with legends –
I mean that give rise to legends – and which the other pictures
must consider with distaste (*La Giaconda, L'Indifférent*, Millet's
Angelus, etc. . . .). Certain books give rise to legends and their
fate is different from that of other books, even if these are a
hundred times finer.

Le Grand Meaulnes is typical of such books. And one of
mine: *Les Enfants Terribles*, shares this strange privilege. Those
who read it and read themselves into it became, through the
fact that they believed themselves to be living my ink, the victims
of a resemblance that they had to keep up. This resulted in an
artificial confusion and the putting into conscious practice a
state of affairs for which unconsciousness is the only excuse.
The works that say to me: 'I am your book', 'We are your
books' are innumerable. The war, the post-war, a lack of liberty,
which at first sight seems to make a certain way of life impossible,
do not discourage them.

In writing this book in the Saint-Cloud clinic I drew inspiration partly from friends of mine, a brother and a sister, whom I
believed to be the only people living in this way. I did not
expect many reactions because of the principle I was affirming.
For who, I thought, will read themselves into this? Not even
those with whom I am dealing, since their charm lies in not
knowing what they are. In fact, they were, as far as I know,
the only ones not to recognize themselves. For from their counter-
parts, if any exist, I shall never learn anything. This book became the breviary of mythomaniacs and of those who like to daydream.

Thomas l'Imposteur is a legend, but it is a book which does
not give rise to legends. During the liberation it all but had
the same effect as *Les Enfants Terribles*. A number of young
mythomaniacs lost their heads, disguised themselves, changed
their names and took themselves for heroes. Their friends called
them *Thomas l'Imposteur* and told me of their exploits, when
they did not do so for themselves. But mythomaniacs who be-

come identified with their own fable are very rare. The others do not like to be unmasked. Moreover, it is very simple. A book gives rise to legends at once or else it never will. *Thomas l'Imposteur* will never share the fate of *Les Enfants Terribles*. What would a mythomaniac make of a mythomaniac? It is like an Englishman playing the part of an Englishman.

The death of Thomas de Fontenoy is mythological. A child plays at horses and becomes a horse. A mythomaniac reads *Les Enfants Terribles*. He plays at horses and thinks he is a horse.

On measurement and Marcel Proust

Perhaps I know to what extent I can go too far. Yet this is a sense of measurement. Of which I have very little. Rather I pride myself on a sense of balance, for this need be no more than the skill of a somnambulist moving along the edge of the rooftops. This leaves me if something wakes me or if, as can happen, through foolishness I wake myself. It is not this sense I am talking about. I am talking about the sense of measurement that perplexes me because it relates to methods with which this book deals, methods which I record without analysing them. I am quite at sea in the world of figures. They are a dead language to me and I do not understand them any more than I do Hebrew. I count on my fingers. If one has to work anything out on paper I am lost. All sums are beyond me. Any calculations I make are resolved as if by magic. I never set them out. I never count my lines, nor my pages, still less my words. When I write a play the act imposes its curve upon me. I have a little trouble over the descent. A click in my mind informs me that it is the end. So far I have never asked myself: 'Is it too long?'[1]

---

[1] Addition from 1st edition. E.S.

Is it too short?' It is what it is. I cannot judge. In practice it turns out to be as it should be.

A film, to be used, must be at least two thousand four hundred metres long. This is not a satisfactory length. It is too long to suit a short story. Too short to suit a novel. No matter. That is the set length. One must keep to it. While I was shooting *La Belle et la Bête* that was the management's great anxiety. I would be too short. In vain I countered this by my own methods; the figures contradicted me and they are law. The film grew shorter. The faces grew longer. I continued to go my own way.

A film is made up of longs and shorts. It has an internal rhythm. Figures do not know this rhythm. The counter's figures were correct. So were mine.[2]

When, on the last day, I questioned my script-girl about the balance between the script (which is one thing) and the action (which is another) she replied, in amazement, that I was right on the mark. I was entitled to two more shots held in reserve. In fact, without knowing this, I had decided the evening before on two further shots. There remained the length of the film, which I refused to extend. End to end, cut up, cut, recut, it had its two thousand four hundred metres. Not one more, not one less.

If I recount this anecdote, in which I appear to have come off so well, it is to give an example, drawn from life, of a victory gained over arithmetic by those figures which dwell within us and work themselves out of their own accord. Poetry is only figures, algebra, geometry, workings-out and proofs. However neither figures nor proofs can be seen.

The only proofs that poets can give are the kind which I record. Accountancy imputes them to some devilish luck. The Inquisition would have made us pay dearly for them.

A long work may not be long. A small work may be big. The measurements that govern them are of our own calculation. *Adolphe* is a big book. Proust is short.

At Marcel Proust's apartment, boulevard Haussmann, the figures which I set against those of the mathematicians were

[2] Do two and two make four? Gustave de Rothschild said: 'Two and two make twenty-two.' And two chairs and two apples do not make four.

proved true. It was their very hive. One could follow their work under a pane of glass. One could almost touch them with one's finger. The cork hood to the brass bedstead, the table crowded with phials, with a theatre-phone (a device enabling one to listen in to certain theatres), with a pile of exercise books and, as on the rest of the furniture, a pelt of dust which was never dusted off, the chandelier wrapped in brown holland, the ebony table on which are piled, in the shadows, photographs of cocottes, of duchesses, of dukes and of footmen of grand houses. The chimney-piece with its tarnished looking-glass, the covers, and that dust and that smell of anti-asthmatic powder, a sepulchral smell, this whole Jules Verne room was a *Nautilus* cluttered with precision instruments for the working out of our figures, our numbers, our measurements, and where one seemed fated to see Captain Némo appear in person: Marcel Proust, slight, bloodless, with the beard of the dead Carnot.[3]

That caliph's black beard – Proust would put it on and take it off as quickly as those provincial comedians who impersonate statesmen and orchestral conductors. We knew him bearded, we saw him beardless, just as Jacques-Emile Blanche portrays him, an orchid in his buttonhole and a face like an egg.

We were talking about Marcel Proust one evening in the presence of my secretary who knew little of the man or his work. 'Your Proust,' he suddenly exclaimed, 'makes me think of the brother of the sequestered woman of Poitiers.'[4] Astonishing remark. It sheds a light on this boulevard Haussmann apartment. One pictures that brother, his big watery eyes, his policeman's moustache, his stiff collar, his bowler hat; he goes into his sister's room and, in the voice of an ogre taking part in a ceremonial: 'Ho! Ho! This goes from bad to worse.' It must have been these words endlessly repeated that the wretched girl distorted in the course of time from her dream and which became

[3] Sadi Carnot, black-bearded President of the French Republic 1887. Assassinated in 1894. E.S.

[4] This refers to a woman who was locked into her room for years by her mother and her brother. When eventually discovered, lying contentedly in a filthy bed among heaps of oyster shells, she never ceased to regret being moved from her 'dear little grotto'. *La Sequestrée de Poitiers, Documents Réunis par André Gide, Gallimard 1930*. E.S.

Malempia. How could one not think of this 'dear deep sanctum' of 'this dear little grotto' in that fusty room where Proust would receive us lying on his bed, dressed, collared, cravatted, gloved, terrified by the fear of a scent, a breath, a window ajar, a ray of sunlight. 'Dear Jean,' he would ask me, 'have you not been holding the hand of a lady who had touched a rose?' – 'No, Marcel.' – 'Are you sure?' And half serious, half in jest, he would explain that the passage in *Pélleas*, where the wind has passed over the sea, was enough to give him an attack of asthma.

Lying stiffly and askew, not among that sequestered woman's oyster shells, but in a sarcophagus of the remains of personalities, of landscapes, of all that he could not use in Balbec, Combray, Méséglise, in the Comtesse de Chevigné, the Comte Greffhule, Haas and Robert de Montesquiou, looking in short, very much as later we were to revere, for the last time, his mortal remains beside the pile of note-books containing his work which, for its part, continued to live to his left, like a dead soldier's wrist watch, Marcel Proust would read to us, each night, *Du côté de chez Swann*.

These sessions added to the noxious disorder of the room a chaos of perspectives, for Proust would start anywhere, would mistake the page, confuse the passage, repeat himself, begin again, break off to explain that the lifting of a hat in the first chapter would reveal its significance in the last volume, and he would titter behind his gloved hand, with a laugh that he smeared all over his beard and cheeks. 'It's too silly,' he kept saying, 'no . . . I won't read any more. It's too silly.' His voice once more became a distant plaint, a tearful music of apologies, of courtesies, of remorse. 'It was too silly. He was ashamed of making us listen to such silliness. It was his fault. Besides he could not reread himself. He should never have begun to read. . . .' And when we had persuaded him to continue, he would stretch out his arm, pull no matter what page out of his scrawl and we would fall headlong into the Guermantes or the Verdurins household. After fifty lines he would begin his performance all over again. He would groan, titter, apologize for reading so badly. Sometimes he would get up, take off a short jacket, run his hand through the inky locks that he used to cut himself and that hung down over his starched collar. He would go into a closet, where the livid light was recessed into the wall. There one would catch sight of him standing up, in his shirt sleeves, a purple waistcoat on the torso of a mechanical toy, holding a plate in one hand, a fork in the other, eating noodles.

Do not expect me to follow Proust on his nocturnal excursions and describe them to you. But you may know that these took place in a cab belonging to Albaret, the husband of Céleste, a night cab truly worthy of Fantômas himself.[5] From these trips, whence he returned at dawn, clutching his fur-lined coat, deathly pale, his eyes dark-circled, a bottle of Evian water protruding from his pocket, his black fringe over his forehead, one of his button boots unbuttoned, his bowler hat in his hand, like the ghost of Sacher Masoch, Proust would bring back figures and calculations which allowed him to build a cathedral in his bedroom and to make wild roses grow there.

Albaret's cab took on a particularly sinister appearance in the daytime. Proust's daytime outings took place once or twice a year. We made one together. This was to go and look at the Gustave Moreaus at Madame Ayen's, and afterwards at the Louvre, Mantegna's *Saint Sebastien* and Ingres's *Turkish Bath*.

To come back to measurements. I linger over describing Proust, because he illustrates my thesis so well. And his handwriting, what does it look like on the pages of those exercise books, which all the members of the *Nouvelle Revue Française* would collate, cut out, paste in, try to decipher, in the rue Madame? Like ciphers as the word decipher indicates.

By dint of adding, of multiplying, of dividing in time and in space, Proust brings his work to a close by the simplest of methods, of casting out the nines. Once more he finds the figures with which his work began. And this is where he captivates me.

For his intrigues have lost some charm, his Verdurins some comedy, Charlus some tragedy, his duchesses some of the prestige of Mesdames de Maufrigneuse and d'Espars. But the structure of his measurements remains intact. Freed from anecdotes

---

[5] 'Hero' of one of the earliest crime-and-mystery serials by Pierre Souvestre and Marcel Allain. E.S.

they interweave. They become the work itself. They are a scaffolding which obscures the monument.

Swann, Odette, Gilberte, Albertine, Oriane, Vinteuil, Elstir, Françoise, Madame de Villeparisis, Charlus, the Queen of Naples, the Verdurins, Cottard, Morel, Rachel, Saint-Loup, la Berma, what do all these puppets mean to me? I see the framework that connects them, the joints of their encounters, the elaborate lace-work of their comings and goings. I am more struck by the interlocking of organs than by that of emotions, by the interlacing of veins than by flesh. My eye is that of a carpenter looking at the King's scaffold. The planks interest me more than the execution.

On haunted houses

You cannot haunt your house at will. It is a question of
storm and fire. There have been times when mine rejected me.
It withheld its assistance. The walls absorbed nothing. They
lacked the great shadows of fire, the sheen of water. The more
my house ignored me, the more I ignored it. This lack of exchange caused a deadlock. No longer could we lay traps for one
another. No trap, no game. That means to live with an empty
bag. My friends felt this. And they withdrew like the walls.
I had to wait for the emanations to return, to counter one
another, to form this explosive mixture which causes our
dwellings to blaze. For they imitate us and only offer us what
we give them. But this echo speaks and insists on dialogue.

Of all my homes Rue Vignon was the most haunted. It was
almost at the corner of the Place de la Madeleine, up under
the roof, and had no pretensions to being pleasant. But there
was flood and fire. I could not describe it. It was its emptiness
that was full. Furniture, objects came there of their own accord.
One did not see them. What one saw was this emptiness, an
attic of emptiness, a dustbin of emptiness, an emptiness full

to the brim. The ghosts queued up in it. The mob stood tight-wedged. There was no floating whatever. A crowd of shadows propped you up. The main body of the army occupied my room. The rest camped right down to the hall and on the stairs. Elbow to elbow. In heaps, in clusters. These on the floor, those on the walls or on the ceiling. Their tumult was a silent one. Guests liked this room. They did not notice anything peculiar except the whole thing. This whole comforted them, put them at their ease, relaxed them, cut them off from the outside. Those invisible people were my responsibility. They saw to the service, hotted up the drama to the right point. Horrors would break out. The emptiness would then make such eddies that one had to cling to some piece of wreckage. But my company would come into action, smother the flames, stamp out the embers.

And tranquillity itself, once it had returned, looked like Phaedra, seated in her chair.

A song of Marlene Dietrich's was often heard there. The one beginning *'Leben ohne Liebe kannst du nicht'*. Recently I was dining at her table. I asked her for it. She sang it to me. The restaurant became my room. It emptied itself, it glorified itself. And the ancient ghosts appeared. And the dead rose from their tombs.

Beside this room and that of Proust and that of Picasso, Rue Schoelcher, which overlooked the Montparnasse cemetery and where the emptiness was inhabited by a mass of objects and forms, I have known haunted houses in which our phantoms played no part. They were haunted by the pleasing craziness of their owners. Their emptiness was full of another sort of emptiness: that of the obsession with emptiness and of a morbid desire to escape from it. The setting here was all-important and the strange appearance of these houses proceeded rather from the presence of things than from their invisibility.

Good taste never produces spectres of this kind and if Edgar Allan Poe had designed a house for himself, doubtless instead of being built on the pattern of his cottages, it would have taken its style from the House of Usher.

If we must have ugliness, I have always preferred to good taste, which depresses me, the violent bad taste of those women who are actresses without a theatre, tragedians without tragedy, and with a physique predisposing them to extravagance. Such was the case of the Empress Elizabeth of Austria, and of Rachel when, too ill, she no longer acted. Then the dreams of such great ladies in quest of dramatic action, materialize and become a setting for them. The one spends her energies on English Gothic, on trapezes, on columns, on plaster mouldings, the other on grottoes and monograms, on tortured bedsteads and on scroll-work anticipating 'modern style', oddly combining Greece with the Synagogue, the face of Antinoüs with a Jewish profile.

The Marquise Casati owned a haunted house. It was not so before it was hers. It was the old Palais Rose which had belonged to the Comte Robert de Montesquiou.[1] The Comte de Montesquiou claimed that it was haunted. Haughty, a stickler for his due, this man who would have wanted both Mohammed and the mountain to come to him, pursued the acme of bad taste, and it repelled his advances. His mauve gloves, his basket of hydrangeas, his air of mystery and arrogance, put it to flight. Did he think he could seduce it or did he realize his efforts were vain? He died embittered and his house became the property of the Marquise.

Luisa Casati was originally a brunette. Tall, bony, her gait, her great eyes, her teeth of a racehorse and her shyness did not accord with the conventional type of Italian beauties of the period. She astonished. She did not please.

One day she decided to exploit her type to the full. It was no longer a matter of pleasing, displeasing or astonishing. It was a matter of dumbfounding. She came out of her boudoir as from the dressing-room of an actress. She was red-haired. Her locks stood on end and writhed round a Gorgon's head, so painted that her eyes, that her mouth with its great teeth, daubed black and red, instantly turned men's glances from other mouths and other eyes. And as they were beautiful the men took in this. They no longer said : 'She is nothing to write home about.' They

[1] At *le Vésinet*.

said to themselves: 'What a pity that such a beautiful woman should daub herself in this way!'

I imagine that her dresses too were the subject of long study. Like the Casati Isis which adorned a room in the Palais Rose and which we saw in 1945 at José-Maria Sert's, she was coated in cloth of gold.

I am reminded of Georgette Leblanc, of her trains of gold and her chasubles, climbing hills on a bicycle behind Maurice Maeterlinck. Artless women, courage personified, marvellous, you loved gold on your fabrics. You could never keep a sou.

As soon as she came out of her dressing-room, the Marquise Casati received the applause usually given to a famous tragedian at her entry on to the stage. It remained to act the play. There was none. This was her tragedy and why her house became haunted. The emptiness had to be filled whatever the cost; never for a moment could one stop bringing down the curtain and raising it again on some surprise: a unicorn's horn, dressed-up monkeys, a mechanical tiger, a boa constrictor. The monkeys developed tuberculosis. The unicorn's horn became coated in dust. The mechanical tiger was eaten by moths, the boa constrictor died. This sinister bric-à-brac defied ridicule. It left no room for it. It reigned in the house of the Comte de Montesquiou. For indeed extravagances are paid for dearly, even in a frivolous world. Montesquiou collected other people's extravagances and in this too he missed the mark. How could I not be reminded of the last scene of *La Fille aux yeux d'or*?[2] Like the Marquise de San Réal, the Marquise Casati, in the midst of the blood of objects and of animals, victims of her dream, adds more black and more red, disguises herself and turns round and round.

May these lines be a tribute to her. I suspect that wherever she is, she carries, embedded between her shoulder blades, the Empress Elizabeth's knife.

For a house to be haunted there must be commitment. The Marquise was committed in her own way. The Comte de Montesquiou was not. For one can commit oneself at any rung of the ladder. From top to bottom.

[2] From *La Comédie humaine* by Balzac. E.S.

Sartre has raised a great hare here. But why does he restrict himself to visible commitment? The invisible commits further. This is to exclude the poets, who commit themselves for no other reason than to lose. My detractors acknowledge in me a freedom that commits me – in wrong directions. I know what they are thinking of. Of opium, of police raids, etc . . . What have opium and police raids to do with this business? Our commitment is a matter for the soul. It consists in not keeping for oneself an iota of comfort.

One haunted hotel was the Hotel Welcome at Villefranche. True, it was we who haunted it, because nothing predisposed it to be so. There was of course the shaded street. There were of course the Vauban ramparts and the barracks which, at night, evoke the absurd magnificence of dreams. There was of course on the left, Nice, on the right, Monte Carlo and their pretentious architecture. But the Hotel Welcome was quite charming and seemed to have nothing to fear. Its rooms were painted with Ripolin. They had put a coat of yellow paint over the Italianate *trompe-l'oeil* of its façade. The bay harboured fleets. The fishermen mended their nets and slept in the sunshine.

It all began with Francis Rose. His mother was clairvoyant. In the dining-room she would get up from the table, approach some gentleman or lady and foretell their future. She wore linen dresses on which Francis used to paint flowers. He was nearly seventeen. Everything dates from the dinner party given for his seventeenth birthday. An armchair draped in red velvet had been prepared for me at the end of the table and a bust of Dante stood beside my plate. Lady Rose had only invited some English officers and their wives. About eight o'clock a strange procession appeared at the bottom of the slope which led from the town to the harbour. Crowned with roses Francis gave his arm to Madame Isadora Duncan in a Greek tunic. She was very fat, a little drunk, escorted by an American woman, a pianist and a few people picked up *en route*. The stupefaction of Lady Rose's guests, her anger, the entry of the procession, the fishermen flattening their noses against the windowpanes, Isadora kissing me, Francis very proud of his crown, that is how this birthday dinner began. A deathly silence turned the guests to stone. Isadora kept laughing, sprawling against Francis. She even rose and led him into a window recess. It was just then that Captain Williams, a friend of the Roses, came on the scene. He had a habit of bringing pigeons and rabbits out of his sweater and his sleeves. He drank a lot. I suppose he had drunk a lot. He was holding a stick. He crossed the room, approached the window and, crying out in a loud voice. 'Hi, you old hag, let go of that child!' he brought his stick down on the head of the dancer. She fainted. Everything dates from that blow with the stick. Our rooms became, as in *Le Sang d'un Poète*, stage-boxes from which henceforth we watched the show, the battles between the sailors from French, English and American ships. Christian Bérard, Georges Hugnet, Glenway Westcott, Mary Butts, Monroe Wheeler, Philippe Lassell lived at the hotel. We drew, we invented, we visited from one room to another. A mythology was born of which *Orphée* sums up the style. Stravinsky was living at Mont Boron. I used to take him the Latin texts of *Oedipus Rex*. He was composing the oratorio as he received them. Those invisible people who come when they will and keep an eye on us, were filling the hotel. They brought to it drama, dizziness, sacred fire.

I am told that of the Welcome Hotel nothing remains but the walls.[3] That is the final triumph of the emptiness. Doubtless it will be rebuilt. But let travellers beware. It is haunted. Ghosts are not killed by bombs.

[3] Inaccurate.

On pain

It would be logical to bear pain better when one is young, since one has a stretch of time before one and the hope of recovery. The pains of my youth, however, made me more impatient than I feel now. Yet I ought to say to myself that I have not much margin left and that if these pains last much longer there is a risk of my never getting rid of them. I take it that my present age is less foolish than was my youth, and that it is not through resignation or fatigue that I bear my complaints better, but through a sense of equilibrium. Perhaps too, having no time to lose, I tell myself that one must overcome the complaint and undertake the work of which it tries to defraud me. Perhaps again, no longer having any use for my person, other than a spiritual one, physical degradation affects me less. The fact is that I have been suffering every minute for the last six months, that I see my ills assuming every shape and form, defying medicine, and yet I remain alert and courageous. Writing these lines relieves me. It can even happen that in giving myself up to my memories, although this book urges me to curb them, I entirely forget my complaint and that I feel as if I were living, not in the room where I work, but in the place and the period I am describing.

It is enough to make me wonder whether, since the work works on us and we are really not responsible for it, it is not just a defence mechanism against sickness which forces me to write this particular book.

I like people whose youth heralds their age and whose structure allows one to visualize the appearance which will one day be theirs. Life sculptures them and perfects them. From a rough sketch they become what they should be and are firmly set in it. I have not had this good fortune. In me, youth is long drawn-out. It becomes spoilt and does not set well. As a result I have the look, either of a young man blundering into old age, or of an old man blundering in an age which is no longer his. Some may think that I hang on to it. This is very far from true. If it is a fine thing for a young man to be young, it is a fine thing for an old man to be old. Moreover, youth should be apparent in speech and in looks. What worries me is this false youth that impels me into behaviour which I far from intend, since I detest sham and if I were able to control my actions, I should play the part of an old man. I dare not confess here, even though I am resolved to tell all, the ingenuousness that shackles me and urges me towards mistakes which a person of my age would never commit. I know nothing of the world. The least learning makes a fool of me, and if my name compels me to attend the lectures of my colleagues, I am ashamed of my inability to understand what is being said. An odd old man who closes his eyes, nods his head, appears to be following the speeches and mutters to himself : 'I am the school dunce.' I scribble on my desk. The others think that I am giving all my attention. I am doing nothing.

From suffering I gain one advantage; it calls me constantly to order. The long periods in which I used to think of nothing, only letting words float around in me : chair, lamp, door, or other objects over which my eyes were roaming, these long periods of vacancy no longer exist. Pain harasses me and I must think to distract myself from it. It is the opposite of Descartes. I am, therefore I think. Without pain I was not.

What will be the end of my torment? Shall I live it to the end? Shall I emerge from it? Are these not the afflictions of age beginning? Are they accidental, these phenomena, or normal? It is this too that saves me from rebellion and makes me bear my complaints in patience. I do not want to add to my absurdities that of believing myself to be a young man, prematurely stricken.

It is possible that I shall wake up one fine day without feeling pain in any limb and I may be utterly mistaken in my prognosis. That would be all to the good, but I prefer to be a pessimist. I have always been one, from optimism. I always hoped too much not to put myself on guard against disillusion.

The doctors had ordered me mountains and snow. This, they said, is the only effective medicine. My germs would disappear as if by magic. I did not believe them. These germs, whether of the animal or vegetable kingdom, are as remote from me as the stars. I feel them. They do not know me. I do not know them any better and the microscope examines me without understanding them, as the telescope examines the sky. They seem, on the contrary, to like high places and the snow. I have already remarked on this. It pleases them that I should breathe, sleep, eat, walk, that I put on weight. They live on me. I am their god whom they torment and Marcel Jouhandeau is right in saying that men make God suffer. Sometimes I say to myself: 'God thinks us. He does not think about us.' And my germs become active. And I suffer. And I think about this. And I tell myself that God suffers by reason of his worlds. That he will so suffer without end.

I can sleep when I am ill. Sleep anaesthetizes me. On waking I think that I am no longer suffering. This lasts for a flash. Another flash brings the pain back where it was. Last night the pain was so acute that sleep did not work. The germs were devouring my right hand. When I touched my face, I felt a crusty mask under which they live and radiate at top speed. Now they have reached my chest. There they are tracing out that red constellation I know so well. I wonder if the sun does not exacerbate this tribe of darkness and if yesterday's sunshine has not something to do with this attack. What an exhausting hunt! What swift game! The doctors prescribe for me weapons that do not kill. Ointments, spirits, vaccines. I give up. Doubtless what is needed is death, that is to say an end to the world.

Apart from the pain, what keeps on nagging at me is the scheme of these creatures in relation to myself. I should like to know how long their centuries last, how many generations succeed one another in them, if they live under a monarchy or a republic, their means of transport, their pleasures, the style of their buildings, the objects of their labours. It is intolerable to be the habitation of a tribe whose customs one does not know. Why last night were they working between the fingers of my right hand? Why this morning do they leave them in peace and toil at my chest, so immensely far from my fingers? Nothing but enigmas of which I am the object and which rub my nose in my ignorance. Perhaps last night I was the scene of a Hundred Years War. One war alone is waged in the world. The world takes it for several. The pauses seem to it to be the normal state of mankind, that is to say peace. Probably the same is true for my germs; that my attacks are long wars and their short periods of rest are peace. From where I view them the war never stops. From where they view themselves there are several wars, quite disconnected, divided by several periods of peace.

Last night I suffered so much that there was nothing but my pain to distract me from my pain. I had to make it my sole diversion and with good reason. It had thus decreed. It attacked at every point. Then it distributed its troops. It encamped. It so manoeuvred that it was no longer intolerable at any one of its positions, but tolerable at them all. That is to say that the intolerable being distributed, it was this no longer, except as a whole. It was something both tolerable and intolerable. The organ that breaks down and the final chord that goes on for ever. A great, full, rich pain, sure of itself. A balance of pain to which I had to get used, cost what it may.

My concern then became to condition myself to it little by little. The least rebellion might excite it and increase its anger.

I had to accept as a privilege its victory, its retinue, its trenches, its tents, its camps, its sleepers, its fires.

At about nine o'clock it ended its preparations: marches and strategic movements. At ten everything was in order. It was in occupation.

This morning it seems to be holding its horses. But the sun is out for the second time since I have been living on the mountain. What to do? Should I avoid this sunlight or use it as a secret weapon against the sleeping army? Should I take it by surprise? Should I let it sleep?

The last time the sun came out I risked the attack. True the germ population was astir. Was it afraid of the red sky which I became for its night? There was frightful chaos on the roads, jostling of men, rearing of beasts. The pain changed its position, became intense, ceased to be so, flew elsewhere. My eyes swelled, wrinkled, made pockets. Under my arms a small tribe seemed to be seeking refuge.

Medicine remains powerless in face of these problems. One must suffer until the warriors slaughter one another, until the race is exhausted, until there is nothing left but rubble. No more than among mankind is there any remedy for this frenzy of destruction.

What is amazing is the dispatch with which my troops move from one end of Europe to the other. What am I saying? From the moon to the earth, from the earth to Mars.

If the germs merely wanted to feed on my body, they would cultivate their farms and not become restive. It seems, then, that they must know the hatreds of patriotism, the pride of great powers, the frenzy for living space – the dole, oil trusts, hegemony. It is impossible for me not to notice the similarities between the menaces in the newspapers of 1946 and the disturbances of which I am the universe. I was speaking of God. Without going as far as him, I pity the world if it experiences what I experience, if it must suffer a return of the canker, when it was hoping for rest.

Yesterday evening and without doubt as a result of the sunshine I had absorbed, the carapace on my forehead began to run, a watery fluid varnished it, made it greasy, and if I mopped it up, it ran harder than ever.

Next my neck began to run in the same way. In the night all this became covered, developing as it dried a follicular crust. My eyes swelled up, above, below, until I could no longer see, and the skin of my face burned as if I had been struck by a back-flash.

These phenomena have kept me awake all night, and in an ineptness in which I was at a loss what to do.

This morning my face is still gilded by the sun, but it seems to be powdered with yellow and under my eyes are deep lines which make a ridge from one to the other.

Moreover I felt torturing pain between the fingers of my right hand. My armpits gave me no peace.

On my neck I have an oozing sore. Such is the catalogue of disaster. I could almost laugh at it, if the incomprehensible and even the miraculous did not always produce in me a disgust that prevents this. All of which does not alter the fact that I am better, that I am benefiting from the height and the food, which is excellent in this hotel. Germs or no germs this army of parasites fights between the derm and the epiderm, near the surface, disfigures me, torments me and does not penetrate. This, at least as far as I can observe, is the site of their manoeuvres, for if they were to penetrate, I can scarcely imagine what ravages they would not cause in my system.

Yesterday, in spite of this upheaval, I wrote some poems. Except for *La Crucifixion*, which I should have written long ago and which was, in a sense, already written inside me, I had not felt any urge to do so. And anyone who has read this book knows that I am most careful not to force the issue. So yesterday it was a surprise for me to feel the urge and not be able to escape from it. The machinery ran easily, difficult though it was, for it was a matter (I was careful not to exert any influence over this) of false internal rhymes, sometimes going from the end of one word to the beginning of another; of almost inaudible sonorities, of very marked peculiarities, of platitudes doubtless apt for throwing them into relief. These poems dealt with the snow which I have before my eyes, but in an allusive form in which it can scarcely be divined.

About seven o'clock at the height of my attack, I tried to distract myself from it and to get on with my harvest. The machinery had ceased to run and actually made fun of me, forcing me to imitate it in a feeble sort of way. I kept quiet and went no further.

Rereading these poems, I am astonished at their complete break with *La Crucifixion*. Verses of a somewhat pedantic nature, because what I am after or think I am after, or what is being dictated to me in large handwriting, is a penance for having allowed myself to be too much seduced by the cinematograph and other frivolous pastimes.

I am never tired of examining that phenomenon in which we appear to be so free and are, if the truth were told, without a shadow of freedom. All the same this shadow exists. It half conceals our work from us. It keeps an eye on us. It holds us balanced between itself and the light, and the word penumbra would suit it better. While I am examining it (or examining myself) I suffer. I have been wrought by this suffering for seven months, as a piece of gold is wrought by a goldsmith. It must surely be putting its tongue out over the task. It did me a good turn. I stirred, therefore I slept. A man of my nature does not bestir himself thus unless he is dreaming. Theatre, drawings, films all were to me pretexts for this constant movement in which one's spirit whirls around, leaving no deposit. I shook my bottle. That is enough to sour the wine.

Suffering has put the brake on me. Despite any efforts to overcome it with fatigue and the giddy round, the day always comes when it orders us to be quiet and keep still. In hospital my eyes were not yet open to this. My poems about the snow, this book about myself, these ink-stained pages, this room of study, instead of the emptiness to which I should have confined myself (medical advice being: think of nothing), are like a good form of silence. That is how I choose to interpret them. This is the only form of 'think of nothing' that I can manage. With this mist and these Alps before me I panic at the thought of having risked another. That prescribed by the doctors.

On death

I have passed through times so intolerable that death has seemed to me a delicious thing. So I have formed the habit of not fearing her[1] and of looking her straight in the face.

Paul Eluard astonished me when he told me he was frightened to see me defying death in the part of the *Baron Fantôme*, in which I dissolve into dust. To live disconcerts me more than to die. I did not see Garros dead nor Jean Le Roy, nor Raymond Radiguet nor Jean Desbordes. My mother, Jean de Polignac, Jean Giraudoux, Edouard Bourdet, are the dead with whom I have lately been connected. Except for Jean de Polignac I made drawings of them all, and was left alone in their rooms for a long time. I looked at them very closely in order to follow their lines. I touched them, I admired them. For death takes trouble with her statues. She smooths away their wrinkles. However much I said to myself that they were not concerned with what concerns me, that sickening distances separated them from me, I felt that we were quite close, like the two sides of a coin which cannot know each other, but are only separated

[1] I have kept 'Death' in the feminine throughout this chapter. E.S.

from each other by the thickness of the metal.

If I were not sad at forsaking the people I love and who can still hope for something from me, I would wait with curiosity for the shadow, worn at the onset of death, to touch and foreshorten me. I should not enjoy the *coup de grâce* and the lengthy business leading up to the point where she has merely to finish us off. I should like to bid farewell to my nearest and dearest and to see my work rejoice to take my place.

Nothing about death disgusts me except the pomp with which it is accompanied. Funerals disturb my memories. At Jean Giraudoux's I said to Lestringuez : 'Let's go. He never turned up.' I imagined him playing at some pin-table in a cellar of the Palais-Royal.

Bourdet's was icy. It was freezing and the photographers climbed into the pulpit to photograph us and flash their magnesium.

My mother's death dealt gently with me. She had no 'second' childhood. She returned to her own, saw me in mine, thought I was at school, talked to me in detail about Maisons-Laffitte and was not troubled. Death had only to smile at her and take her hand. But the Montmartre cemetery, which is ours, offends me. They park us like motor cars. The drunks who cross the bridge piss down on us.

Yesterday I visited a mountain cemetery. It was under snow and had few graves. It had a commanding view of the Alpine range. Ridiculous as it seems to me to choose one's last resting-place, I thought of my hole in Montmartre and I felt sorry not to be able to be buried here.

After the death of Jean Giraudoux I published a farewell letter which ended : 'I shall not be long in joining you.' I was taken to task for this remark which was considered pessimistic, bearing the stamp of despondency. It was nothing of the kind. I meant to say that even if I am to last until I am a hundred it is only a few minutes. But few people are willing to admit this or that we are whiling away our time playing cards in an express which is hurtling towards death.

Since Mother Angélique[2] dreaded death at Port-Royal, who

[2] Angélique Arnauld, 1591-1661, Abbess of the Abbey of Port-Royal. E.S.

then will find it a blessing? As well await death without flinching. It is flattery to think of nothing but her, ungracious to apologize for living as if life were a mistake of death's. What will those people say who imprison themselves in a cell and anxiously examine the documents of their trial? The Court will give them no credit for doing so. It has already reached its verdict. They will only have wasted their time.

How admirable the attitude of one who has made good use of the time granted him and who did not interfere by trying to be his own judge.[3] Duration of human life belongs to those who mould each moment, sculpture it and do not trouble about the verdict.

On the subject of death there is still much for me to say, and I am amazed that so many people are troubled by her, since she is within us every second and should be accepted with resignation. How should one have such great fear of a person with whom one cohabits, who is closely mingled with our own substance? But there it is. One has grown used to making a fable of her and to judging her from outside. Better to tell oneself that at birth one marries her and to make the best of her disposition, however deceitful it may be. For she knows how to make herself forgotten and to let us believe that she no longer inhabits the house. Each one of us houses his own death and reassures himself by what he invents about her – namely that she is an allegorical figure only appearing in the last act.

Expert at camouflage, when she seems to be furthest from us, she is our very joy of living. She is our youth. She is our growth. She is our loves.

The shorter I get, the longer she grows. The more she makes herself at home. The more she bestirs herself about this and that. The more she devotes herself to trivial details. Less and less does she take the trouble to deceive me.

But her glory is when one ceases to be. She can go out, and she locks us in.

---

[3] It needs the thundering genius of Chateaubriand for me to endure Rancé. (Abbé Armand de Rancé, reformer, 1626-1700. E.S.)

On frivolity

Frivolity is a crime in that it apes lightness, that for instance, of a fine March morning in the mountains. It leads to that disorder, invisibly unclean, worse than any other disorder, fatal to the harmonious functioning of the constitution (like eczema) through the almost pleasurable itch induced on the derm of the intelligence, by the *fantaisiste*, that rascal so readily confused with a poet.

If you consult Larousse you will see there that Rimbaud is a *poète fantaisiste*, and there is a certain redundancy in the intent of the one guilty of this insertion. For most people a poet is necessarily a *fantaisiste*, unless the most dubious lyricism or bogus profundity earn him a respect that matches his vapidity.

Frivolity is nothing but a lack of heroism and a kind of refusal to give oneself away in any respect. It is a flight mistaken for a dance, a slowness seeming a swiftness, a heaviness appearing like this lightness of which I am speaking and which is only met with in souls that are profound.

It may happen that certain circumstances, for instance Oscar Wilde's imprisonment, open the criminal's eyes to his crime and force him to repent of it. Then he will admit that 'all that is understood is right, all that is not understood is wrong,' but he only admits it because he is made aware of it by discomfort. The same is true of Pascal's accident in his carriage.[1] One cannot imagine without horror a spirit of his quality in love with itself and with life to the point of attaching such extraordinary importance to being saved from death.[2]

I accuse of frivolity anyone who is able to apply himself to solving problems of local interest without the least sense of absurdity, a sense that might make him think, and direct his efforts towards a peace, for instance, instead of a war. For unless he is criminally frivolous, this dangerous person only finds excuses in personal interest, whether for profit or for fame. And patriotism is a poor excuse, since there is more nobility in displeasing the masses who are its dupes than in duping them in the name of greatness.

Frivolity, already odious when it works on a superficial level, since there are in that field heroes of a charming lightness spoilt by frivolity (certain Stendhal characters among others), becomes monstrous when it proliferates to the point of tragedy and, through the easy charm it exerts over all lazy minds, entices the world on to ground where true seriousness seems like a childishness which must give way to the circle of grown-ups.

So one has to witness, helplessly, all that frenzy of catastrophes, of red tape, of controversies, of murders, of trials, of debris, of murderous toys, at the end of which the hideous frivolity of man comes to itself again, dazed, stupefied, in the midst of a disorder as when children slash pictures, put moustaches on busts, throw the cat into the fire and upset the bowl of goldfish.

True, frivolity soon raises its head again, not wishing to

[1] It is said that the mind of Pascal was affected as the result of this accident. E.S.

[2] I know very well it's a matter of dying in a state of grace or not. But then how I like the following story. At dinner with Stravinsky, his son Theodore told us that at a luncheon party of free thinkers in New York, a guest had died while insulting the Blessed Virgin. 'He is lucky,' said Stravinsky, 'for he went straight to heaven.' His son asked him why. And Stravinsky replied : 'Because he died of shame.'

believe itself guilty under any circumstances. This is the stage
at which the family bickers in a corner of the drawing-room
while the furniture is being removed, when feverish grievances
prevent its members from noticing that the pieces of furniture are
disappearing one after the other and that there is not even a
chair left to sit on.

What irritates me is the person whom everyone expects in advance will please me because he is a *fantaisiste*. Phantasy and
frivolity are wedded, I repeat. The *fantaisiste* incapable of originality, find this in the annoyance he causes you by the lack of co-
ordination in his behaviour. He wants to astonish. He is a hind-
rance. He thinks himself a marvel. He does not move any of
the pawns that are the opening of a game. He contents himself
with mixing up the dominoes and the cards, placing the chess-
men in positions unsuited to the mechanics of the game, but
suited to catch out the players at first glance. He treats times,
places, conventions with an insolence which is not even that of
the dandy and without ever interrupting his course for the sake
of anyone else. He numbs and bludgeons, like the drunkard
when he imposes upon us the superiority he feels, from the height
of which he despises what he takes for our conventionality,
and which is merely our embarrassment.

I have known *fantaisistes* in whom phantasy was as it were
organic and who died of it. I felt in them a kind of mild madness very dangerous both for themselves and for their friends.
Despite the respect which all existence that does not spare
itself inspires in us, none the less they fill us with uneasiness. For
these *fantaisistes* are usually mythomaniacs, and sometimes their
aim is to hold not our attention but our hearts. If they succeed
in this, it means that they are neither frivolous nor given to
phantasy, but that they appear so because of their clumsiness
in convincing us, from a modesty of spirit which impels them to
try to appear exceptional, from a desire to enter into our scheme
of things from their remorse at having thought themselves in-
discreet. This remorse inveigles them into flights, into total
eclipses, into punishments which they inflict upon themselves
and of which I could quote appalling instances.

The world in which they live makes contact with them very

difficult for us, since the least word, the least gesture on our part (and which we thought of no significance) sets in motion in them incredible deviations which may lead them even to suicide.

One must therefore shun them from the beginning however much they may beguile us in a world where fire is rare and never fails to attract us.

I have not observed this caution often enough. I considered it unworthy and belonging to a self-indulgence I do not allow myself. Some scruple would make me afraid to slam my door in the face of an unknown guest. I would open it and dare not afterwards change my attitude, so great was my shame at appearing pusillanimous. And that is what is so serious. Instead of swiftly foreseeing the effects of a weakness prejudicial to my surroundings and to my work, I prided myself on defying the traps and jumping into them with both feet. So I behaved in this way more from pride than from natural generosity. And for this I blame myself.

I mentioned the dandy. One must not be misled by those who saw in his attitude, taken as a means to an end, a visible image of their own haughty spirit and of their rebellion. I understand how Baudelaire would feel the attraction. He goes the other way round. This dramatist is himself a drama. He is drama, theatre, actors, audience, the red curtain, the chandelier. A Brummel is, on the other hand, the perfect male counterpart of the *tragedian without a theatre*. He will act his part in a void, until he ends up in the final void of a garret where he dies while having all the great names of England announced to him. His comment: 'I cannot have been well dressed at the Derby, since you remarked on it,' takes on its full meaning when Baudelaire is reduced to depending upon an article in which Sainte-Beuve admires in his work only a sonnet to the moon. 'His head hot and his hand cold,' says Goethe somewhere. The dandy has a cold head and a cold hand. I advise ships to avoid this insolent iceberg. Nothing will change his course. He would commit murder for the sake of tying his cravat. Moreover, his imperialism has no foundation. He is only anointed by himself. One fine day Brummel asks King George to rise and pull the bell-cord. This bell is enough to wake the rightful king from his brief hypnosis and he shows the king of fashion the door.

When kings show poets the door, the poets win. When the King of England shows Brummel the door, Brummel is lost.

Our era is very sick. It has invented 'escapism'. The horrors afflicting the victims of the frivolity of a war amply provide it with certain outlets. It dopes itself through the medium of its newspapers and even the atomic bomb is the occasion for a kind of Jules Verne lyricism – until the moment when a practical joker pulls their leg over the radio. Orson Welles announces the arrival of the Martians. A French broadcast, that of a fireball. Whereupon our supermen no longer think of escaping with their minds but with their legs. They wear them out. They take to flight. They faint. They abort. They call for help. To such a degree that the government is disturbed and forbids the fictitious broadcast. One would think that poetry would soothe them and carry them right away from the hideous reality. This is what they do think and what is exploited by a vast number of magazines, whose smallest advertisement sets ajar the doors to dreams.

The poet was alone in the midst of an industrial world. Now he is alone in the midst of a poetic world. Thanks to this world, as generously equipped for escapism, as it is for winter sports, by the theatres, the cinematograph, the glossy magazines, the poet at last regains his invisibility.

On the Palais-Royal

The disorder against which I am fighting recreates itself slyly around me bit by bit. Probably my internal and external crop – soul, hair, eye-teeth, all pointing in every direction, does not end with my person but continues to the extreme limits of its carapace, which limits must extend far beyond my view.

This carapace is so conditioned to live upon our essence that it is the victim of the afflictions that torment us and grows sick with our skin. The ill from which I suffer, in face of which medicine admits itself powerless, communicates itself to the objects and paraphernalia in my room, maddens them and makes their bric-à-brac assume the strange postures of insomnia and of pain.

These pains are like stigmata responding to certain needs of my work. Whether it be *Le Belle et la Bête* assailing me in those places where the film compels me to torment an actor with hair and spirit-gum, whether it be an arrow shot at this same actor becoming a shot from the projectors on to my eyes, whether it be the recasting of the script of *Le Sang d'un Poète* resulting in an intolerable attack on my right hand. Last night,

at the end of my resources against this attack, I kept shaking
my hand as hard as I could, and I perceived that this was what
the poet does when he is trying to rid himself of his wound
which is a mouth.

Here am I then in a bed, itself tortured with rucks and
bumps, for in tossing from eve till morning I cause a
turmoil.

From this bed of sorry state I gaze upon my room, a narrow
cabin opening on to the arcade of the Palais-Royal, framed
by the sound of footsteps. This room has so often been described
by journalists, magnified by photographers, that I ask myself if
this is really it, so little does it resemble what they portray. That
is to say that the journey of what is seen, between the eye
through which it enters and the hand through which it emerges,
must change the breath into a strange sound, as happens with
a hunting-horn. About the red it is difficult not to agree.
For the rest I suppose that the objects that are only mine in
some haphazard way, must have taken on in the eyes of the
journalists, the appearance of what they expected to find,
rather than what they really were. They were looking for the
store of stage properties for my legends. In fact these objects,
the only ones to succeed in remaining in a house from which
everything goes, have nothing in common but a peculiar intensity
distinguishing them from thousands of other finer ones the col-
lectors possess. The most engaging bits of such wreckage, thrown
up on this little red beach, is without doubt the Gustave Doré
group of which the Charles de Noailles gave me a plaster cast
from which I had a bronze made. In it Perseus is to be seen
mounted on the hippogryph, held in the air by means of a long
spear planted in the gullet of the dragon, which dragon is
winding its death throes round Andromeda. This group is on
a column standing between the so-called *castor* window and a
tall piece of slate that can be moved aside and that conceals
a small room which is too cold to be used in winter. It was there
that I wrote *Renaud et Armide,* away from everything, set
free from telephone and door bells, in the summer of 1941, on
an architect's table above which one sees saved from my room
in the Rue Vignon where it adorned the wall-paper, Christian

Bérards' large drawing in charcoal and red chalk representing the meeting of Oedipus and the Sphinx.

The slate door and several others in the hall enable me to jot down in chalk addresses and work to be done, for I have a memory like a sieve. Visitors of a romantic disposition think they are looking at hieroglyphics, rather than at an aid to memory which I sponge out every week.

On the right of my bed are two heads, one Roman, in marble, of a faun (this belonged to my Lecomte grandfather), the other of Antinoüs, under a glass dome, a painted terracotta, so fragile that only the steadiness of its enamel eyes can have led it here from the depths of centuries like a blind man's white stick.

A third head adorns that of my bed: the terracotta of Raymond Radiguet, done by Lipschitz, in the year of his death.

Here is a list of the pictures hanging on the walls above the flood of disorder: Lithographs for *Faust* by Eugène Delacroix. Photographs of Rimbaud by Carjat, taken on the day of the sword-stick scandal. Collage by Picasso in a butterfly box. Portrait of Sarah Bernhardt by Clairin (she is a sculptress). Original by Bérard for the cover of *Opéra*. Large figure of a woman by Picasso in Indian ink. Photograph of Mallarmé with his shawl. Picasso's die (see the end of *Potomak*). Sketch by Ingres for *Tu Marcellus eris*. Profile of Baudelaire, dry point by Manet. My portrait done in Rome by Picasso in 1917 and dated Easter Day. Two pen drawings by Victor Hugo. One of Gavroche. Victor Hugo wrote under it: 'Watching the guillotine.' The other is a finicky attempt at his monogram. A graceful watercolour of my mother by Wencker.

The rest smothered under the paraphernalia, the books, the unanswered letters, the bottles of medicine and jars of ointment with which they smear me, is nothing but the seaweed from my storm, the remains of the innumerable apartments and hotels where I lost those treasures they stole from me and of which nothing remains.

I rented this tiny cellar, wedged between the Palais-Royal Theatre and the block of houses ending in the Comédie-Fran-

çaise, in 1940, when the German army was marching on Paris.
I was then living at the Hotel Beaujolais, next door to Colette,
and was not to settle in at 36 Rue de Montpensier until 1941,
after the exodus. The friends to be near whom I had somewhat
rashly rented this odd tunnel had had to flee from the premises.
The Berls, the Milles and the Lazareffs. I lived here for four years,
subjected to insults, aimed at my work and my person. I tend
myself there for the moment through weariness, because of the
impossibility of finding a suitable dwelling and also because of
a charm (in the exact meaning of the word) which the Palais-
Royal casts on certain spirits. This charm is made up of the
ghosts of the revolutionaries who haunt it, of a silence adorned
with birds, following the *fêtes* of the Directoire, of an almost
Chinese setting, as of a dead city between the ramparts of very
old squalid houses, bending like the palaces of Venice where
Delphine de Nucingen would lead Rastignac to the gaming
rooms.[1]

There I know everyone, their habits, their cats, their dogs.
There I walk among the smiles and the news we get from one
another. There I eat in those little cellars to which one descends
by four steps. There I meet my friends and the ghost of Giraudoux, who came from elsewhere but was one of us. From my
window I gossip with Colette, as she walks across the garden
with her cane, her silken cravat, her flat felt hat, her fine eyes,
her bare feet, her sandals.

I shall not like to leave this room and yet I shall have to.
A harsh wind is driving me to this. I shall miss, wherever I go
into the sunshine, my twilight. I shall miss the theatre lights
which the winter snows reflect to me from below. And the
sight I saw the other day (among a thousand others): the hair-
dresser near the Galerie de Chartres, had put out his wigs to
dry in the sunshine. These wigs were stuck on waxen heads
and those heads on the points of the spikes of the railings which
at night enclose the ghosts of Thermidor.

The gates, opening in the morning on to crossroads, passages, vaulted ways, lamps, colonnades, arches, dovecots, perspectives of Russian squares, Roman cities, cellars, kiosks selling

[1] from *La Comédie humaine* by Balzac. E.S.

postage stamps, books about flagellation, the Légion d'honneur, it is there one plays *boules* under the trees, it is from there that heads used to roll into the gutters, heads that were the *boules* of a popular game, and it is there that the processions of ragged ruffians used to file past, brandishing them like fists at the stone-framed sky.

On the rule of the soul

We cannot run from place to place without losing something, suddenly move all our goods from one place to another and change our work all in a moment just as we please. Nothing takes so long over its journeys as the soul, and it is slowly, if it detaches itself, that it rejoins the body. Hence those who think themselves speedy are thrown into confusion, badly reassembled, since the soul, joining them little by little and having rejoined them when they departed, is found by them to perform the same exercise in reverse. In the end they come to believe that they are, and are no longer.

The same thing applies to the discomfort of passing from one work to another, since the finished work goes on living in us and only leaves a very confused place for the new work. It is important, in regard to a journey, to wait for the body to reassemble itself and not to rely on an appearance in which only those who do not know us well can have any faith.

In regard to one's works, it is important to wait after each one, and let the body free itself of the vapours which remain in it and which may take a long time to disperse.

Hence the danger of a work for the cinematograph like the one I have just finished, for the hypnosis it subjects us to is such that it is difficult to tell where it ends. Even when the film detaches itself from us and having consumed us, circulates with an unconcerned life of its own, more remote than that of the stars, our machine remains subject to it and will not shake it off.

I have fled from a house, driven away by doorbells and telephone bells. I am living in a countryside where silence, birds, plants, flowers take the place of domestic disorder.[1] But I do not flatter myself that I am yet where I am or that I am free there. Only a small part of me profits from it. Not only have I had to conquer, in order to move from prison into fresh air, the same disgust as if the opposite were happening, for our habits, whatever they are, have a hold on us, but also one half of me decided to flee and the other half to stay where it was. With the result that I have to wait for myself and be patient until the moment when I shall have rejoined myself. In my estimation it takes a month, after a work or a journey to regain control of one's individuality. Until then it is in limbo. Only just enough of me is left to loaf about the garden, contemplating the absurd genius of flowers and recalling certain remarks about them, for instance that of Guez de Balzac, when he tells how a Norwegian peasant, who had never seen roses, was astonished that shrubs should bear fire.

Such sights pass through me without leaving any imprint. They enter, they leave, I eat, I go to bed, I sleep.

Each time I find myself in this intermediate state, I wonder if it is permanent. It upsets me to the point of making me exaggerate the void it creates and convinces me that it will never be filled. It is then that exercises would work marvels. A whole course of gymnastics calculated to get a lazy mechanism going again. But I dare not aspire to that. There things remain a riddle for us as much as animal, vegetable, seed or egg.

Here I am then between two rhythms, unbalanced, weak in body and lame in mind. Woe to him who rebels against this. An attempt to bypass it would only make things worse. And do not tell me that it is of little importance, that if this task of

[1] Verrières.

setting things in motion again is madness, you will destroy it. Nothing that is done can be destroyed. Even if one burns it and nothing of it remains but ashes.

For if the detailed execution of our labours gives us the illusion that we are free, the completed work gives the lie to such freedom. It is the whole that gives it its inevitable form, like a plant putting forth its flower.

This is why I spoke of 'absurd genius', genius that man, whether he likes it or not, has in common with the plants – and willy-nilly, unless he throws himself into confusion by his own act, the man who has it must in some way be absurd – and without the pride of flowering.

This is my method of waiting, and my anguish disgusts me, since it is hardly likely that plants set themselves such problems as would exhaust and etiolate them.

What is one to do against this fear of emptiness? It dries me up. One must forget it. I practise doing so. I go to the point of reading children's books. I avoid any contact which might make me aware of the passing of time. I vegetate. I talk to dogs.

To be aware that within oneself are such mysteries is not conducive to comfort. Therefore one's discomfort, the uneasiness it causes and the resulting wear and tear do not by any means cease with the work. A new kind of torture begins and not a minor one, the torture of the desert, of mirages and other cruel phantasmagoria of thirst and lingering echoes. Until the good fortune of a new discharge that consents to make use of our machine again, to take advantage of it, to set it going once more, bringing in its train a whole apparatus of ferocious egotism and total indifference to pain.

Make sense of it if you can. Try to break the chain. Imagine you can cut it short other than by dying at the end of it.

Far be it from me to complain. I accept this penal servitude. No doubt it suits me so well that, if I were to escape from it, I would reconstruct it somewhere else.

I have been ill now for a year. It seems that in the neutral state I am now in, the disease is less interested in injuring me. It wants me whole, attentive. What can the doctors do? What do they know of these cells, indifferent to the individual they constitute? These cells think, without any regard for my interests. They construe them in their own way and show a knowledge of psychology.

If I tried to unravel this skein, where should I be? Far better – this is my theory and I stick to it – to daydream.

You are daydreaming, I say to myself. You are foretelling the future. I boast. In fact, I am returning to the forsaken places of my loves. Under the pretext of analysis I pay a call on myself. It is the *Tristesse d'Olympio*. Here is the path where the merchant sees the Beast spring out of the thicket, here is the ruined gateway that Beauty pushes open and through which she sees the Beast drinking. Here are the candelabra that light themselves, the arms of living stone that move them and come out of the walls. Voices pursue me: *'Beauty, will you be my wife? – No, Beast. – Farewell then, Beauty. Until tomorrow.'* Or: *'Does it not disgust you to give me a drink?'* or *'Beauty, if I were a man, I would assuredly do the things you bid me, but poor beasts who wish to prove their love can only lie down on the ground and die.'* And I can see the Beast. His poor eyes, one larger than the other, swimming, drowning. They roll, showing their whites. Beauty will love him and lose him. Out of this great caterpillar springs the Prince Charming. And the prince asks: *'Are you happy?'* and Beauty replies: *'I shall have to get used to it.'*

Will the film rolled up in its boxes at Saint-Maurice let go of me? Doubtless the children of our minds are dependent upon us until their marriage with the public. Must I drag on until September, when this marriage will take place?

One ghost expels the other. My play which should be staged in October is so far away from me, so foreign, that it reproaches me. It looks coldly into my eyes. It poisons me. It will surely take its revenge in its own time. It increases my discomfort with the anxiety it holds for me. It hates me but it humours me. It still has need of me.

Thus I mix the paste in which I get stuck. In so doing I am in danger of getting more stuck than ever. The spectacle of nature which should distract me plants me more firmly in it. Moreover my refuge is a park where I once planned to make my actors move. And without my thinking about it, this plan that I had forgotten had something to do with my choice of a dwelling where I hoped to find peace. Its setting superimposes itself on those I used. Their trees grow entangled. Their brambles overlap. Their thickets part. The Beast appears. He devours me. I am lost.

The legs of my soul being stuck deep in this mire, I sometimes envy those writers who use a table and put up a barricade. They do not allow their ink to treat them with familiarity. If they involve themselves in writing, they behave with great caution and only involve a part of themselves in what they write.

The part that they keep for themselves has legs, so that it is apt to inspire respect, indeed withdrawal if necessary.

Woe to him who has not kept a plot of ground on which to live, a small piece of himself within himself, and is open to hazards that take advantage of the smallest rail to grow brambles on. For if no rule is observed, they will creep in both from without and from within. That is why this vacancy, to which I give myself up, bound hand and foot, is dangerous, and why I should be more strict than anybody in guarding my doors. This is what paralyses me. They enter who will, the quick and the dead. I said, earlier, that images and words passed through me with impunity. That is easily said. I stated later that nothing goes through us without leaving imprints on the sand where the eighteen feet of the Muses will only walk if it is virgin.

Who can daydream and pay enough attention to his fences to forbid any access to his domain? One knows what notices warning people of savage dogs and wolf-traps are worth. One must therefore accept the inextricable and submit to it to the point when a certain charm arises from it and the jungle becomes endowed, through its wild innocence, with the attractions of virginity.

The truth is I am lost in it. The last recourse left to me is in moral progress. For all that, however, the jungle must not become an untidy heap of rubbish and nettles.

That is the only battle that I wage against myself, in which I am able to remain in command.

On Guillaume Apollinaire

Instead of tormenting myself with any pretentious quest, since the powers that drive me must have a view quite other than my own about the use to which my capacities should be put – and if they know nothing about me, which is likely – they must be as alien to them as electricity is to a box and to the tunes of a radio – I would do better to use my sick pen to portray the splendid people I have known. People are always asking me to do this and wanting me to add a sequel to *Portraits-Souvenir*. I am reluctant to do so for the good reason that I have recorded in this events of my youth in which I was a mere spectator, without being in the least implicated. Later I come in to play. It is a tournament. I am wounded and I wound. And I shall wound much more severely if I dig into the scars. It is very seldom that one does not displease those one describes, and even if we do not twist their actions to our advantage but to our disadvantage, the optics and the perspective of the fixed point where we stand are at variance with the angle from which they observe them. They make us appear dishonest.

To this is added the fact that memory is distorting (concave or convex), that the smallest anecdote becomes distorted from mouth to mouth, that if we tell one, it returns to us in travelling kit, that the most realistic person is susceptible to the seduction of legends and believes them loyally; that by a phenomenon of inverted perspective, memory has a tendency to see things growing larger as they move further away, to get them out of proportion, to remove their bases, in short that nothing is more suspect than evidence.[1] I have known eye-witnesses whose evidence, based on error of vision, would without demur have sent an honest man to the guillotine, and who, when their inaccuracy was proved, would embroil themselves further rather than feel any shame. It is certain that the flight of time casts a spell because in it reality twists itself in a manner that shocks a mind untutored in the realm of art, but fascinates it when the events are romanticized.

Hence the success of collected letters, memoirs and other direct testimony in which we can touch the myth as we read an interview, an article, the paragraph of the Larousse dictionary which concern us.

A cult of speed does away with craftsmen to such an extent that the patience, the manual dexterity essential for the creation of the best, is no longer found except in those who adapt mechanics to such a purpose. Reading was once a craft. It is falling into disuse. People rush. They skip lines. They look at the end of the story. It is therefore normal for the hasty to prefer memories of facts that give rise to works to the works themselves, and absent-mindedly to swallow the tools, through weariness at having to chew what they carve. This is also why people prefer conversation to the written word, because it can be listened to with half an ear and demands no effort.

Conversation thus becomes dangerous. I have never known

[1] There is nothing more dangerous than the words that are attributed to us and which are circulated and printed. I read in a preface of a book by Bernanos, written in Brazil, a remark of mine that I never uttered and that shocks me. The Word is always and instantly made flesh. That is why what is said has incalculable consequences. That is why it is important to take care what is hawked around, to verify the sources and, if they are false, to cut it clean out.

good ones in which people showed any concern for one another. Whatever is said, faulty listening distorts it. A new haste prevents those to whom it is recounted from telling themselves that this is not our syntax. The signature blinds them. They believe in it. They retort. The retort goes off on its travels. It is travestied *en route*. Confusion without end.

Misunderstandings of this kind are innumerable. This is why I should like to note down a few memories of a man with whom, because he was considerate to the point of mania, I never had any disagreement.

I mean Guillaume Apollinaire.

I knew him in a pale blue uniform, his head shaven, one temple marked by a scar like a starfish. An arrangement of bandages and leather made him a kind of turban or little helmet. One might have thought that this little helmet hid a microphone by means of which he heard what others cannot hear and secretly surveyed an exquisite world. He would transcribe its messages. Some of his poems do not even translate its code. We would often see him listening in. He would lower his eyelids, hum, dip his pen. A drop of ink hung upon it. This drop would tremble and fall. It would star the paper. *Alcools, Calligrammes* – so many cyphers of a secret code.

François Villon and Guillaume Apollinaire are the only two I know of who steer a steady course through the limping measures of which poetry is made, and which is not suspected even by those who think they are producing poetry because they write verse.

The rare word (and he certainly used it) lost, between Apollinaire's fingers, its picturesqueness. The commonplace word became unusual. And he would set those amethysts, moonstones, emeralds, cornelians, agates which he uses, wherever they came from, like a basket-maker plaiting a chair on the pavement. One cannot imagine a craftsman more modest, more alert than this soldier in blue.

He was fat without being obese, his face pale and Roman, a little moustache above a mouth that uttered words in a staccato voice, with a slightly pedantic grace and a kind of breathlessness.

His eyes laughed out of his solemn face. His priest's hands accompanied his speech with gestures recalling those used by sailors when drinking a glass and then pissing.

His laugh did not come from his mouth. It came from the four corners of his being. It would invade him, shake him, set him jerking. Then this silent laughter would drain away through his eyes and his body would regain its poise.

In socks, without his leather leggings, his short breeches clinging to his leg, he would cross his little room on the Boulevard Saint-Germain, climb a few steps to the minute study where we made the acquaintance of the edition de luxe of *Serres-Chaudes* and of the brass bird from Bénin.

The walls were covered with his friends' canvases. Besides the portrait of Rousseau with the hedge of carnations and Laurencin's angular young girls, there were *fauves*, cubists, expressionists, orphists and a Larionov of the machine period of which he used to say: 'It's the gas meter.'

He was mad about 'schools' and had known, since the days of Moréas at the Closerie des Lilas, the true source of the names they bear and that people cryptically repeat.

His wife's face was like one of those pretty bowls of goldfish in the little shops on the quay, opposite the bookstalls with which, he once wrote, the Seine is shored up.

The morning of the armistice of 1918, Picasso and Max Jacob had come to 10 Rue d'Anjou. I was living there with my mother. They told me that they were anxious about Guillaume, that fat had developed round his heart and that we must telephone Capmas, my friend's doctor. We called Capmas. It was too late. Capmas begged the invalid to help him, to help himself, to exert his will to live. He no longer had the strength. The charming breathlessness became tragic. He was suffocated. That evening, when I joined Picasso, Max and André Salmon in the Boulevard Saint-Germain, they told me that Guillaume was dead.

His little room was full of shades and shadows: those of his wife, of his mother, of ourselves, of others, who drifted around, gathered together and whom I did not recognize. His dead face lighted up the linen surrounding it. Of a laureate beauty, so radiant that we felt we were looking at the young Virgil. Death, in Dante's robe, was leading him, like a child, by the hand.

While he was alive his corpulence was not noticeable. The same was true of his breathlessness which was not really breathlessness. He seemed to move among very delicate objects, on ground mined with goodness knows what precious explosives. A strange gait, almost as if he were walking under water, which I was to find a trace of once more in Jean Paulhan.

This air of a captive balloon gave him a certain resemblance to the character Sunday in Chesterton's *The Man who was Thursday* and to the Roi Lune in *Le Poète Assassiné*.

This could still be seen in his remains which, though unmoving, soared. This essence of elder trees, of birds, of dolphins, of everything that repudiates weight, was freeing itself from his corpse, raising it, making in contact with the air a phosphorescent combustion, a halo.

Once more I saw him sauntering through the streets of Montparnasse, dotted with the white markings of hopscotch, carrying about him that store of fragile things of which I have spoken, avoiding breakages and uttering learned remarks. For instance that the Bretons were originally Negroes, that the Gauls did not wear moustaches, that *groom* was a corruption of *gros homme*, as pronounced in London, where the Swiss doormen, emulating France, were later replaced by little boys.

Sometimes he would stop, lift a finger of a marquise and say (for instance): 'I have been rereading *Maldoror*. Youth owes far more to Lautréamont than to Rimbaud.' I quote this remark among a thousand others, because it reminds me of what Picasso described to me: Picasso, Max Jacob, Apollinaire, all young, rambling about Montmartre, running down its steps, and shouting: 'Long live Rimbaud! Down with Laforgue!' a 'meeting' a thousand times more significant in my opinion than those which precede plebiscites.

One morning in 1917 (Picasso, Satie and I having just weathered the scandal of *Parade*), Blaise Cendrars rang me up to say that he had read in the revue *Sic* a poem signed with my name, which he was surprised that he did not know, that this poem was not in my style and that he was going to read it to me over the telephone, so that I might confirm that it was not by me. The poem was a fake. Over this fake Apollinaire made quite a rumpus. He exercised a jurisdiction in the world of letters and attached importance to his position. From café to café in Montmartre, from newspaper office to newspaper office he interrogated, suspected and accused everybody, except the guilty party who, much later, confessed his hoax to us. This had consisted in sending a poem to Birot, the editor of the review *Sic,* and baiting it with my signature, in such a way that he would print it without checking it, for this poem was an acrostic; its capital letters spelled the words: PAUVRE BIROT.

Here am I sliding down the very slope that I deplore. So I will describe, as this can offend no one, the evening which ended the first performance of *Mamelles de Tirésias* at the Renée Maubel theatre.

Apollinaire had asked me for a poem for the programme. This poem, the title of which was *Zèbre (Zebra),* used the word *rue* in the sense of *ruer (to kick).* The cubists, headed by Juan Gris, thought that this *rue* was a street and, that evening after the show, demanded an explanation of what this street was doing there. It did not fit in.

At this tribunal, where we appeared side by side, Apollinaire changed over from the role of judge to that of culprit. For having entrusted Serge Férat with his sets and costumes, he was accused of having compromised the dogma by a flavour of caricature. I was fond of Gris and he of me. Everyone was fond of Apollinaire. But if I record this incident it is because it shows on what pinpoints we were balancing. The last prank was suspect, led to inquests and ended in convictions. It was 'I' – Gris would say – 'who introduced the siphon into painting.' (Only bottles of *anis del Oso* were allowed.) And Marcoussis, coming out of the exhibition of Picasso's *Fenêtres* at Paul Rosenberg's, declared: 'He has solved the problem of window fastenings.'

Do not laugh. It is a great period and a noble one, in which in saying that a government that would punish a painter for such niceties can absorb the mind. And Picasso is quite right making mistakes in colour and in line would be a great government.

To come back to our poet. The penal session of *Les Mamelles de Tirésias* left him somewhat bitter. For a long time he remained attached to it by a kite-string. He became a kite. Light, struggling, shaking this string, hollowing himself out, weaving from right to left. He'd tell me he was 'fed up with painters'. And he would add : 'they are beginning to bore me with their architectural diagrams.' Amazing words in the mouth of one who was the originator of a victory over realism. But in this he wanted the sweep of Uccello and for painters to browse in that field poisoned with autumn crocus.

Except for Picasso, that eagle with ten heads, sovereign master in his kingdom, the cubists went as far as measuring the object. Yardstick in hand they compelled it in a humdrum way to serve them. Others brandished tracings, figures, the Golden Mean. Others erected mere scaffoldings.

Apollinaire went round their groups and was exhausted by them.

No doubt this weariness was the beginning of the decline that led him towards death. Nothing pleased him but exquisite surprises. He would complain. He pitied his generation, sacrificed, he said, falling between two stools. He would take refuge with Picasso, who never exhausts himself. He did not suspect for a moment, so true it is that genuineness is unconscious of itself, that he would soar away and become a constellation.

This constellation takes the shape of his wound, wound that a canvas of Giorgio de Chirico prophesied for him.

That is how things happen in our sphere. Everything unfolds according to a mathematical formula unacknowledged by mathematicians, which is our own. There is no stumbling at the last. Yet everything stumbles from end to end.

On that rock where soon only a few of us, escaped from shipwreck, will be left, Apollinaire sings. Beware, commercial traveller ! It is the Lorelei.

There can be no question here of a study. That is not what I have undertaken. I limit myself to a few lines which trace an outline, catch a pose, pin down the living insect, like that profile of Georges Auric in which I produced the likeness by the position of the eye, which is nothing but a dot. Others will analyse Apollinaire, his magic, based as it should be, on the virtue of herbs. He used to collect herbs from the Seine to the Rhine. The concoctions he made, stirring them with a spoon in a mess-tin on a spirit lamp, bear witness to the attraction exercised upon his episcopal self by sacrileges of every kind. One can imagine him equally well on his knees, serving the mass of the regimental chaplain, as presiding at some black mass, removing shell splinters from a wound, as sticking needles into a wax figure. On the Spanish Inquisitor's seat as at the stake. He is both Duke Alexander and Lorenzaccio.

On laughter

The ability to burst out laughing is proof of a fine character. I mistrust those who avoid laughter and refuse its overtures. They are afraid to shake the tree, mindful of the fruits and birds, afraid that someone might notice that nothing comes off their branches.

Like the heart and like sex, laughter functions by erection. Nothing swells it that does not excite it. It does not rise of its own accord.

This excitement is subject to the same rules as that of the senses, for what makes one person laugh does not make another laugh. And I know those who burst into fits of laughter at the same time as myself, while some others who are there only make grimaces, cannot understand us and sometimes imagine that it is at them that we are laughing.

The automatism of laughter is ruthless. It often happens that laughter torments us during funeral ceremonies where it is officially frowned on.

Bergson attributes the cruel laughter at the sight of a fall to the break in the balance which dehumanizes man and changes him into a puppet. Other philosophers contradict his theory. They hold that man, on the contrary, accustomed to his artificial mechanism, is de-puppeted by the fall and suddenly shows himself as he is. It is, they say, this rude discovery of man by man that provokes the laughter.

What vexes me is that neither the one nor the other carry their theory as far as the study of laughter at works of art. The shock of new works, causing a rupture between its customary outlook and the novelty with which it is faced, makes the public stumble. So there is a fall and laughter. This perhaps explains the laughter of crowds which, except by tears or insults, have no other way of expressing themselves.

I like jokes, but they must be long and realistic. If I invent names, places and events, I want them to be credible and pull their weight. I thoroughly enjoy playing this game with skilful players. The family I live with is given to laughter.[1] It excels in such exercises of the mind. It abandons itself to them without reserve. As a result, many visitors take their fiction for fact and, without realizing it, help in their own mystification.

If a third person knows the rules, interferes and goes astray, in short if he indulges in *banter*, I freeze and wish the game would stop. For playing is not banter and funny stories do not make me laugh. They are worth nothing unless they take their natural place in the conversation. Nothing is more rare than for a circle to amuse itself and not confuse cleverness and idle nonsense.

As a rule everyone jumps to right and left, up and down. Everyone mixes things up and all talk at once. That is why I keep to the circle to which I am accustomed and which uses the same vocabulary as myself.

One of the last times I happened to dine with muddle-headed people, my neighbour talked to me of *La Duchesse de Langeais*, a film of Giraudoux's based on Balzac, which was being shown at the *Biaritz*. As I mentioned Balzac, this lady told me I was mistaken, that the film was not being shown at the *Balzac* (a cinema at the corner of the *rue* Balzac), but at the *Biarritz*.

One lives much of the time with one's head under one's

[1] The Vilmorins.

wing. One is reluctant to admit the degree of lack of culture and the mental disorder in which people flounder. As a precaution when walking through the crowd one uses a somewhat blind eye and a somewhat deaf ear. But fashionable society splashes us with mud and throws us down in the mire. So it is unhealthy to frequent it. For we come home wretched, besmeared from head to foot, disheartened to the marrow of our bones.

Stupidity dismays and does not invite laughter. Rather it saddens and makes us stupid by contact with it. We do not relax and stretch to our full capacity except with people who can return the ball. I like to talk. I like to listen. I like people to talk to me and to listen to me. I like laughter that gives off sparks when struck.

I remember a summer at Trie-Château, at the house of Madame Casimir Périer (Mme Simone) with Péguy, Casimir Périer and Alain-Fournier who was writing *Le Grand Meaulnes*. We were convulsed with laughter until we got cramp, and when we were going to bed a word would set it off again, would throw us down on to the stairs leading to our rooms. It clutched us by the belly until the small hours.

I am a very good audience. At the theatre, at the cinematograph, I cry or I laugh without my critical mind being roused. Nothing disgusts me if some force shakes me, shoulders me, makes me let myself go.

On the other hand my critical mind exerts itself over works which attempt to stir other regions in me, which are not those of laughter nor of tears, and whence tears spring to the eyes through the sole gift of beauty.

I have great debates with myself and long periods in which I accept myself for what I am. This is one I am now passing through. Although I go off at a tangent it is none the less true that I come full-circle. What would become of me without laughter? It purges me of my disgust. It ventilates me. It opens my doors and windows. It beats my upholstery. It shakes my curtains. It is the sign that I am not quite sunk by contact with the vegetable world in which I move.

Although I know, from films about plant-life, that the serenity of nature is a myth, that only its rhythm, different from

ours, makes us believe in that serenity, that a garden is continually a prey to eroticism, to vice, to anxiety, to anguish, to
hatred, to agitations of every kind, and that it *lives on its nerves*,
I acknowledge that it has not the gift of laughter.

It is Dante's *Inferno*. Each tree, each bush, shudders in the
place assigned to it, in torment. The flowers it puts forth are like
fires one lights, like cries for help.

A garden is ceaselessly fertilized, corrupted, wounded, de-
voured by great monsters equipped with armour, wings and
claws. Its enemies mock at the artless weapons with which it
blindly bristles. Its thorns give us a proof of its fears and seem
to us more like permanent goose-flesh than like an arsenal.

I have seen a cultivated orange tree at Pramousquier, on
Cap Nègre, lose its head. It was living in sunshine. A palm
threw shade on it. This shade terrified it. On the four branches
shaded by the palm it put out long thorns. It became wild again.
The palm was cut back. The branches calmed down and became cultivated once more. The prickles disappeared. The
following year I found them smooth like the rest of the bark.
So much for fear.

I assure you that this orange tree did not laugh and that,
even when delivered from the suspect shade, it had no desire
to laugh.

If seed is sown it is another generation of the plant that
springs up. If a cutting is taken, the same plant is prolonged to
infinity. (It starts again from youth.) Why cannot an element
be discovered comparable to the soil, that would allow man to
be perpetuated, since the whole individual, look, voice, gait, is
present in the least of his cells, so that if one of his nail-parings
were to be planted he would take birth from it and begin
again from the beginning. It is because everything has to be
paid for. Plants pay for this privilege of not dying by the torment
of occupying such a mean space, of their static condition, of
cramp, of the lack of liberty (relative) to move about, which
man possesses and pays for very dearly by the knowledge of the
small stretch he is given to cover and by death.

In certain species, the tree does its own 'layering'; it lets a branch hang down to the ground and from this branch is re-born in another age, but exactly the same. Thus these species avoid the intervention of man. If they could, they would laugh. For laughter is a great privilege which we have.

Our consciousness is lightened by laughter. Its lightness con-soles us for having such heavy soles to bear us to the scaffold. False solemnity detests it because it enlightens us about the soul. It strips it like a stroke of lightning. I once happened to hear, through a door, the laughter of someone against whom nothing had put me on my guard. This dreadful laughter re-vealed to me a person whom I was one day to unmask.

Laughter can work inversely and a person whom we find antagonistic may conquer our antipathy by a burst of childish laughter.

I know an extremely interesting story about uncontrollable laughter. In 1940, Germany was sending its youth to the arma-ment factories. A young man from Essen, working at Krupp's, was given the sack because he kept having fits of laughter. They moved him to other factories. He was thrown out of them all because he laughed. He was not punished. No other fault could be found with him. They got rid of him. They sent him home with this chit which I saw in 1946: *Incurable frivolity.*

To kill laughter in man is a crime. That is what happens when one involves him in political problems that make him take himself seriously and when he is consulted about things of which he knows nothing. He can no longer laugh. He gives himself airs. It is also what happens when he is not consulted and is beaten into submission.

Pierre Roy, when I ask him about his political opinions, declares: 'I am a moderate anarchist.' I wonder if he has not found the right formula and if France is not entirely committed to this shade of opinion.

On being without being

I must now take my bearings in this house where again I try
to sleep. I have cut off all correspondence with Paris. My letters
are opened and only the essential ones are brought to me. I do
not communicate with anyone. My nettle-rash, on the other
hand, is waking. I notice once again that it likes to thrive and
takes advantage of my vegetating. My arms, my chest, my forehead burn. Doubtless, as the origin of this complaint is the
same as that of asthma, I am incurable and can only hope
for ups and downs. I avoid the sunshine in which I liked so
much to be. I edge along it in the shade. The rest of the time I
shut myself in. I read and I write. Solitude forces me to be
Robinson Crusoe and his island, to explore inside myself. I
bring to this no understanding, for I have none, but a certain
boldness that stands me in its stead.

Incapable of following a trail, I proceed by impulses. I cannot
follow an idea for long. I let it escape when I ought to creep
up and leap upon it. All my life I have hunted in this manner,
for want of being able to do better. That is what deceives
people who take my strokes of luck for skill, my mistakes for

strategy. Never has any man been surrounded with so much misunderstanding, with so much love, with so much hatred, for if the person they believe me to be annoys those who judge me from afar, those who come near me are like Beauty when she dreads a monster and discovers an amiable beast who only wants to reach her heart.

I must say that my dearest friendships spring from this contrast.

The legend surrounding me keeps fools at a distance. The intelligent find me suspect. What is left for me between the two? Strolling players like me change their pitch more often than their shirts and pay by a show for the right to stay where they are. That is why my solitude never appears uncommunicative. I only show myself at the times of the parade before the show, or before my own number. I apologize for this to those who share my caravan and who conclude that I am holding the worst in reserve for them, for they only witness my misery.

Like all vagabonds the obsession for property torments me. I am looking for one in the country. When I find one, either the landlord refuses to sell it, because my enthusiasm opens his eyes to it, or he wants too much for it.[1]

In Paris I find nothing that suits me. The apartments I am offered intimidate me. I want them to say: 'I was waiting for you.'

By dint of counting on the impossible I put down roots in my hole.

'*Je sens une difficulté d'être.*' Thus did Fontenelle,[2] the centenarian, reply when he was dying and his doctor asked: 'M. Fontenelle, what do you feel?' Only his belonged to his last hour. Mine has been from the beginning.

---

[1] Since these pages were printed I have bought the house which was waiting for me. I am correcting these proofs there. I am living in this retreat, far from the bells of the Palais-Royal. It gives me an example of the absurd magnificent stubbornness of the vegetable kingdom. I rearrange the memories of former countrysides where I used to dream of Paris, as later I used to dream in Paris of taking flight. The waters of the moat and the sunshine reflect on the walls of my room their false shimmering marbles. Everywhere spring is jubilant.

[2] Bernard Le Bovier de Fontenelle, writer, nephew of Corneille. E.S.

It must be a dream that one can live at ease in one's skin.
From birth I have had an ill-stowed cargo. I have never been
trimmed. Such is my balance sheet if I prospect within myself.
And in this lamentable state, instead of keeping to my room, I
have knocked about everywhere. From the age of fifteen I have
never stopped for a moment. Sometimes I meet this or that
person who addresses me intimately, whom I cannot recognize
until a firm grasp of the hand unexpectedly drags out of the
shadows the whole setting of a drama in which he played his
part and I played mine, and which I had completely forgotten.
I have been involved so deeply in so many things that they slip
from my memory, and not just one, fifty. A wave from the
depths brings them back to the surface for me with, as the Bible
says, *all that in them is.* It is incredible how few traces are
left in us of long periods which we had to live through in
detail. That is why when I dig into my past, first of all I unearth
a figure – with its earth still clinging to it. If I search for dates,
for sayings, for places, for sights, they overlap, I add things, I
bungle, I advance, I draw back, I no longer know anything.

My great concern is to live now in a way that is right for me.
I do not boast that it is more expeditious than another,
but it is more to my taste. This present of mine abolishes time
to the point of letting me gossip with Delacroix and Baudelaire.
It allowed me, when Marcel Proust was still unknown, to consider him famous and to treat him as if he had achieved the
glory he was one day to enjoy. Having discovered that this
state of being outside time was my privilege, that it was too late
to acquire better ones, I perfected it and plunged even more
deeply into it.

But suddenly *I open one eye* : I realize that I was using the
worst system for thinking of nothing, that I was exhausting
myself with trivial occupations that bind us and eat us up, that
I was busying myself with too many things. I persisted in this
mechanically; I was a slave to it to the point of confusing a
legitimate instinct of self-defence that prompted me to rebellion
with detestable fidgets.

Now I know the rhythm. As soon as I open one eye, I close
the other and take to my heels.

On words

I attach no importance to what people call style and by which they flatter themselves that they can recognize an author. I want to be recognized by my ideas, or better still, by the results of them. All I attempt is to make myself understood as succinctly as possible. I have noticed that when a story does not grip the mind, it has shown a tendency to read too quickly, to grease its own slope. That is why, in this book, I turn my writing around, which prevents it from sliding into a straight line, makes one revise it twice over and reread the sentences so as not to lose the thread.

Whenever I read a book, I marvel at the number of words I meet in it and I long to use them. I make a note of them. When I am at work this is impossible for me. I restrict myself to my own vocabulary. I cannot get away from it, and it is so limited that the work becomes a brain-twister.

I wonder, at every line, if I can go any further, if the combination of these few words that I use, always the same ones, will not end by seizing up and compelling me to hold my peace. This would be a blessing for everyone, but it is with words as with numbers, or with the letters of the alphabet. They have the faculty of rearranging themselves differently and perpetually at the end of the kaleidoscope.

I have said that I am envious of other people's words. This is because they are not mine. Every author has a bag of lotto cards with which he must win. Except in regard of the style I deplore, of which Flaubert's is typical – too rich in vocables – the styles I like, that of Montaigne, Racine, Chateaubriand, Stendhal are not lavish with them. One would not take long to count them.

That is the first thing to which a teacher should draw the attention of his class, instead of extolling fine rhetoric. They would soon learn how richness exists in a certain penury, that *Salammbô* is nothing but *bric-à-brac*, *Le Rouge et le Noir* a treasury.

Words rich in colour and sound are as difficult to use as gaudy jewels and bright colours in dress. An elegant woman does not overdress.

I am astonished by those glossaries in which the notes at the foot of the page, claiming to elucidate the text, remove its point and iron it out flat. This is what happens with Montaigne, whose sole aim is to say what he means to say and who achieves this, cost what it may, by twisting the phrase in his own way. To this way of twisting the phrase the glossaries prefer a vacuousness as long as it flows easily.

This is not to condemn the exceptional use of a rare word, provided that it comes in its proper place and enhances the economy of the rest. My advice, therefore, is to admit it if it does not sparkle too brightly.

Words should not flow : they are set in. It is from a grotto in which the air flows freely that they draw their vigour. They demand the *and* that cements them, to say nothing of the *who, that, which, what*. Prose is not a dance. It walks. It is through this walk or manner of walking that one can tell its breed, that poise characteristic of a native carrying burdens on her head.

This makes me think that elegant prose takes on the function of the burden which the writer carries in his head and that all the rest derives from some kind of choreography.

Once I used to try to share the liking I had for a certain kind of prose with people who claimed to be insensitive to it. Read aloud, with the fear of not convincing them, such prose exhibited its blemishes.

Failures of this kind have put me on my guard. I came to distrust what had at first charmed me. Little by little, I trained myself not to get enamoured of any but the writers in whom beauty dwells without their being aware of it and who are not obsessed by it.

Although the words of a vocabulary may not tally with our own, I sometimes come across a professional term and adopt it. I will quote one which is found in text-books: 'in my estimation'. This says perfectly what it means to say and I adopt it, not knowing any other that suits me better.

The French language is difficult. It rejects certain *douceurs*. It is this that Gide described so wonderfully when he calls it a piano without pedals. One cannot blur its chords. It functions unaided. Its music is addressed more to the soul than to the ear.

What you consider to be musical in the classics is often only an ornament belonging to their times. The great do not escape this although they rise above it. In minor ones the artifice is apparent. Célimène and Alceste[1] seem to us to speak the same language.

It is likely that the most diverse languages we write in our epoch will be indistinguishable in another. They will appear almost similar in style. Nothing will stand out but the difference between what they express and the accuracy with which they express it.

Beyond the fact that words have meaning, they are endowed with a magical virtue, a *spell-binding* power, an hypnotic quality, a fluid that works apart from the meaning they possess. But it only works when they are grouped together and ceases to work if the group they constitute is merely verbal. The act of writing is therefore subject to many compulsions: to intrigue, to express, to bewitch. Bewitchment, that none can teach us, since it is our own and since it is necessary for the chain of

[1] from *Le Misanthrope* by Molière. E.S.

words to resemble us in order for them to be effective. They take our place when all is said and done, and must make up for the absence of our looks, our gestures, our progress. They can therefore only act on people open to such things. For the others it is a dead letter and will remain for them a dead letter away from us and after our death.

The magical power of such word-grouping makes me able to converse with a writer of any period. For they bring me into his presence. I question him. Their internal framework enables me to understand what he would have replied to me. Unless I find the answer all written out as does sometimes happen.

My book has no other object than to engage in conversation with those who read it. It is the opposite of a lecture. My guess is that it would teach little to those around me. It only wishes to meet unknown people who would have liked to know me, and to discuss with me those enigmas in which Europe is uninterested and which will become the murmurings of a few rare Chinese mandarins.

The grouping of words is so effective that philosophers, whose world order is driven out by the next one (and so on) are not remembered for what they said but for their way of saying it. Which one among them does not owe his fame to his writing or at least to the particular light that he throws upon some error? We know now that Descartes is mistaken and we read him all the same. It is the word therefore that endures, by a presence it encloses, by a flesh it perpetuates.

Let me be clearly understood. I am not speaking of the word that decorates a thought. I am speaking of a word-architecture so individual, so robust, so perfectly true to the architect, that it preserves its efficacy even through a translation.

The phenomenon of Pushkin is that he cannot communicate in any language but his own. His *spell* works on the Russians, whatever their opinions. Such a cult cannot depend only on a certain kind of music, and since the sense reaches us without savour there must be magic in it somewhere. I ascribe it to a drop of black blood he had in his veins. Pushkin's drum speaks. Change the beat, the drum alone remains.

True, with poets the part played by words is more active than in prose. But I consider that some intention passes from one language to another if the knot of the words is strong enough. Shakespeare proves it. That is why the case of Pushkin seems to me unique. Twenty times I have had him translated for me. Twenty times the Russian who was doing it would give up, telling me that the word *meat*, used by Pushkin, no longer meant *meat*, but put its taste into one's mouth and that this belonged to him alone. Now the word *meat* is just the word *meat*. It cannot transcend itself except through the words that surround it and make it stand out so strangely.

Vanity counsels us to send our pollen to the stars. But, come to think of it, a poet's luxury should be to belong to none but his fellow countrymen. Doubtless what seemed to me to tell against Pushkin is, on the contrary, what protects him and makes him worthy of the Russian cult of which he is the object.

Prose is less subject than poetry to recipes for spells. True, the further it moves away from the anecdote, the more hazardous it becomes to transfer it to another idiom. Unless there were to occur the providential meeting between a Charles Baudelaire and an Edgar Allan Poe. That is to say between two men equally versed in the use of herbs, spices, drugs, doses, brews, mixtures and in the effect that these produce in the human system.

On youth

I like to consort with youth. I learn from it far more than from age. Its insolence and its severity subject us to cold douches. It keeps us healthy. Besides, the obligation to have to set an example to it forces us to walk straight. I understand how many of our contemporaries shun this contact which I seek. It is tiring because it is always at the ready and does not seem to know what it wants.

Childhood knows what it wants. It wants to emerge from childhood. The trouble starts when it does emerge. For youth knows what it does not want before it knows what it does want. But what it does not want is what we do want. It consorts with us to enjoy the contrast. When it does actually want something, it often happens that I know about it sooner than it does itself. My ears − like those of a circus horse − recognize the music. I score a point.

I remember how Radiguet used to pull out of his pockets weapons to fight us with. I turned them against myself. This is what happens with the young people I come across. I am supposed to be giving to them and it is they who give to me. I owe them everything.

Nothing more idiotic than the motives imputed to my liking for youth. Their faces attract me for what they express. This kind of beauty inspires nothing but respect.

I ask no respect in exchange. In my home youth is at home. I may say that there it forgets my age, which surprises me as much as if I were received as an equal by the Hierophants of Memphis.

Erik Satie, Max Jacob shared this privilege. I was always meeting them arm in arm with young people.

The youth of which I speak is that of capital cities, already clear-sighted. It does not mistake its ground. It finds itself a family with a tradition of anarchy. It adopts it. It digs itself in. Then it shows its ingratitude. It waits to be strong enough to assassinate the family and set fire to the house.

Provincial youths use other methods. They write to us. They complain. They call for help. They want to escape from one social circle to another able to understand them and to help them. If they arrive on foot from Charlesville (because they are still influenced by Rimbaud-ism) they soon find their place.

It would therefore be absurd to expect gratitude from young people and to take pride in the fact that they seek refuge with us. They like us to the extent that they learn from our faults, that our weaknesses excuse their own, that our weariness puts us at their mercy. It is up to us to profit from this medley of reactions and to gain as much from them as they gain from us. Our work is but a slipper for them. They only use it to cut their teeth on.

It is ridiculous to regard youth as a myth and as all of a piece. Conversely, it is ridiculous to fear it, to address it from behind a table, to slam the door in its face, to flee at its approach.

Of course it is mythomaniac. Of course it takes liberties. Of course it eats up our time. So what?

Naturally it ties us up in a network of lies. Naturally it puts on a mask as soon as it comes near us. Naturally it disparages us right and left, and if it takes a false step holds us responsible.

We have to run these risks for the simple reason that young people of this kind reassure us by proving that they are innocent of guile and are passing on the secret of their fire.

Many young people have confessed to me, after a long time, that they came to see me, either as the result of a wager, or because they had read my name on a placard, or in order to disobey their families.

Their silence demoralized me. I embroidered it with a thousand reasons. It was merely due to their fear of talking nonsense.

This does not prevent me from falling into the trap again. For youth intimidates us because we imagine it to be secretive. This is the strength of its silence. We furnish it out of our own pocket. It soon realizes this, and uses it as a weapon. Its silence becomes systematic. Its aim is to put us out of countenance.

It is important to be on one's guard. When the young people have gone, this deathly silence sinks deep into us and works havoc. We, its victims, find in it a criticism of what we are doing. We weigh it up. We agree. We are disgusted. We grow paralysed. We fall from the tree, open-beaked.

I see some artists who are exposed to this adventure losing their footing, incapable of regaining their balance and unable to do without their tormentors.

I am sometimes much astonished at the solitude of our young monsters. When they leave our homes they loaf about in the streets. They complain of not meeting anyone of their own age who suits them. Some of them come to us from the countryside where they live. They do not admit this. They linger. They miss their train. We see them to the door without realizing their position, and that they can neither pay for an hotel, nor return home. They then look so peculiar that I sometimes fear they will drown themselves. What is to be done? They are silent. Impossible to rescue them from a hole they are digging for themselves, from a fall to which their terrible strength of inertia would drag us too.

But they know that all doors are not closed to them, that I am aware of their anguish, that I listen to them, that I talk to them if they do not talk, that I give them little hints. In short, it is an evening snatched from the void in which they are searching for themselves. That moment between childhood and youth is the worst. I have said so before.

Let each of us remember our own drama. Mine was belated and no laughing matter. My dice were loaded. I was proudly leading in my game of snakes and ladders. I had to return to my point of departure and tag along behind.

Encounters that we might have made and did not make might have saved us our stake. We are for youth, perhaps, one of such encounters.

Alas, to reply to all the letters of appeal, to receive all the callers in despair is impossible. That would amount to being chairman of the Suicide Club. Let us beware of the drowning who cling to us and who drown us.

To reply is to attract a letter which demands an answer and so it goes on. To cut this short is to appear contemptuous. It is better not to reply and, if we open our doors, only to allow those whose faces bear a sign of some kind to come again.

This is not the least of the dangers.

Why do young students fail in their duty and what is this duty? I will tell them. They should be the army of the mind's great adventure. How could they understand this? Their conformity blinds them. What conceals it from them is a bogus anarchy, a superficial anarchy, without the shadow of a policy, and which they do not hesitate to put into action against the noblest enterprises. Their ignorance, coupled with the pride they take in it – for they deem themselves infallible – the pleasure too of creating a rumpus (the only word for it) sets them at loggerheads with themselves without their noticing it. By booing at courage they boo at themselves and side with their families whose judgments they disdain.

Moreover the past disgusts them. Classical works only mean for them hours of detention, soiled books, impositions. No young person thinks of rubbing off the dust to rediscover the living work beneath. In that case he would be amazed to find that Racine (among others) under cover of his conventions conceals a terrifying intensity. Instead of going in a gang to the theatre to sneer at his tragedies, the young would set about the actors who distort them. It is the opposite that happens. A bad tragedian can make youth forget its mocking attitude. It acclaims his faults.

Here then are the deaf young, blind to what used to be done, to what is being done, to what is about to be done. What have they got left? A disorder. A hiatus which they fill by organizing demonstrations, marching in file, parading placards, shouting their slogans. So now we are alone if we have to fight. We are without our shock troops. And they even turn against us.

The Abbé Morel told me about his lecture on Picasso at the Sorbonne. He was showing lantern slides of some of his work. The young students, who were packing the hall, kept on sneering, stamping, hooting. Without any break the Abbé showed some masterpieces of Romanesque sculpture. His audience thought they were Picasso's. They hooted, stamped, jeered. The Abbé bided his time and rubbed their noses in the mire. Now these young people, adept at hoaxing and who credit artists with that same skill, greatly appreciated the trap they had been caught in and applauded their hoaxer.

Not one of these young people was capable of taking the floor, of conquering Picasso with new weapons, that is to say of countering him with a living force more living still, of running faster than the Abbé Morel, of turning round and making a frontal attack on him.

I hasten to say that it is not in my power to measure the capacity of each Faculty to come to our aid. I suppose that the Faculty of Science is more localized in the matter of problems, keener on accurate research than the Faculty of Letters. Richer in research than in teaching. I suppose too that the professors of the Faculty of Letters must be to blame, save for the excuse that if they try to stimulate the mind of a class, they give up in the face of its slackness in getting out of the rut.

In any case I am continually struck, although I am aware

that politics are their main interest, by how little the students react – or how badly.

I do not ask the impossible. It is not a matter of long research outside the curriculum, nor the *nuances* of a political system to which we are inured. I ask of the students an untutored impulse towards the unusual and that they shall reflect what Jacques Rivière said : 'there is a time for laughing at others and a time for others to laugh at you.'

M. Bergeret was a wise man when, after the reading of M. Roux's symbolist poem, he held his hand silently between his own for a long time. *He was afraid of wounding beauty as yet unknown.*

It is not such parliamentary caution that I wish for in the students. I should like them to show a lack of caution and to extol what shocks them. I know professors more youthful than they are.

Once when I was to speak at the Collège de France, I first paid a visit to the Dean. I went up to his office, slowed down by the memory of innumerable rebukes. I found a charming and very young old man. 'Beware of our students,' he said to me. 'They only like to note down dates and not to be disturbed.'

So I shook them up. It is a good method. They remember nothing but a jolt. But this jolt does daunt them for a moment.

To sum up. I am not so mad as to expect a crowd of students to know, by magic, what cannot be taught. I would like them to abstain from proudly cutting off their antennae, like the hairs of a first beard. They would be the gainers were they attuned to the electrifying waves that beauty propagates. Even at random.

On beauty

Beauty is one of the wiles that nature uses to attract beings towards one another and ensure their support.

She[1] makes use of it in the most disordered manner. What man calls vice is common to all species whose mechanism works blindly. Nature attains its ends at any cost.[2]

We can hardly imagine the springs of such a mechanism among the stars, since the light which exposes them to us is the result either of reflection or, like all light, of decomposition. Man imagines that they serve him as so many chandeliers, but he sees them only waning or in extinction.

It is certain that the rhythm of this great machine is a cruel one.

The most tender of lovers collaborate in it. The suck of the vampire lingers corrupted in their kiss, a rite representing the

[1] I have referred to Beauty throughout this essay in the feminine. E.S.

[2] Bitches mount dogs. Cows mount each other. This disorder is sometimes an order. The natives of the islands made it a rule before the missionaries came. It was a matter of avoiding over-population.

appropriation of the blood of the person loved, the making of an exchange.

This desire for the blood of others is even more strongly expressed when the lips suck the skin to the point of becoming, as it were, a cupping-glass, and attracting the blood to it and leaving a bruise, a mark that adds exhibitionism to vampirism. This mark proclaims that the one bearing it, usually on the neck, is the prey of somebody who loves him to the point of wanting to tear out his very essence.

As for flowers, they remain the simple snare they were from the beginning. I study them in a testing garden where species are crossed. The glory with which we invest them, for them does not exist, since their colour and scent serve only to make their presence known to the carriers of love.

If we forget our size, we can picture these knights (the insects) in the vast, cool, fragrant rooms of a translucent palace.

The *arum maculatum* holds the knight captive, thanks to a kind of portcullis arrangement, until he is daubed with sperm and the women's quarters are opened to him.

I would have a splendid time spreading myself on this subject. But have I not already said that this book would not become a course of lectures?

I am rather more interested in the similarity of these erotic displays. The world is simpler than our ignorance gives it credit for. It becomes more and more apparent to me that the mechanism works rather crudely, here and there and everywhere.

Beauty in art is a stratagem that she uses to immortalize herself. She travels, she pauses on her way, she fertilizes human minds. Artists provide her with a vehicle. They do not *know* her. It is by them and outside them that she pursues her mission. Should they try to get hold of her by force, they only produce an artifice.

Beauty, simple servant of a nuptial system, oblivious of herself, battens on a painter, for instance, and will not let him go. This often leads to disaster for the progeny of certain creators who claim to procreate in a carnal way and play a double role.

Let no one think that beauty lacks a critical faculty nor that she is proof of one. Neither the one nor the other. She goes straight to the point, whatever that may be.

She always seeks out those who espouse her, thus ensuring her survival.

Her lightning, striking the high points, sets fire to works that shock. She shuns banal representations of nature.

The cult of the banal representation of nature is so deeply rooted in man that he loves it, even in painters for whom it only serves as a springboard. When this representation, painted with equal precision, offers him anecdotes from dreams or from imagination, he rebels. Such an anecdote no longer concerns him but concerns *another*. His egoism rejects it. He sits in judgment. He condemns. The crime is to have tried to distract him from his self-absorption.

Just as people do not read but read themselves, he does not look, he looks at himself.

Art comes into existence the moment the artist departs from nature. What makes him depart gives him the right to live. This becomes a *La Palice* truism.[3]

But the departure can occur indiscernibly. (I am thinking of Vermeer and of certain very young modern painters.) That is to reach the height of art. There beauty slips in by stealth. She sets a perfect trap, as innocent-looking as a plant's. She will slyly lure people to herself without rousing the fear that her Gorgon's head always does arouse.

Diderot exasperates me when he describes Greuze's anecdotes in detail. Baudelaire would aggravate me by describing those of Delacroix were he not fertilized by this painter. Dante set the trap for Delacroix. Delacroix set the trap for Baudelaire. The phenomenon can be seen with the naked eye in the Delacroix-Balzac fertilization (*La Fille aux yeux d'Or*).

From century to century the Giaconda lures a swarm of gazers into those traps that Leonardo believed he had laid solely to catch the beauty of his model.

[3] Jacques de Chabannes, 1470-1525, Seigneur de la Palice, Maréchal de France. Later a song perpetuated the legend of his ingenuousness giving rise to the expression *une verité de la Palice*. E.S.

At the cinematograph, every film, thanks to the absence of colour, escapes the commonplace and accidentally enjoys the privilege of a work of art. Beauty ventures there as rarely as possible. Colour will ruin this ambiguity. All will be ugly but the beautiful.

People shun coloured films because they do not find them close enough to nature. Once again it is in its very divorce from it that colour will reign and that beauty will make use of it.

The reproductive instinct urges the poet to scatter his seeds beyond his boundaries.

I repeat it : poorly transmitted, they fructify. Certain species (Pushkin) refuse transmission. But this does not prevent them from scattering at large and even when reduced to insignificance, from fructifying.

Shakespeare remains the model of the explosive plant. His seeds have taken advantage of wings, and storms. Beauty is hurled across the world on tongues of fire.

Were we able to measure the distance separating us from those whom we believe to be nearest, we would be frightened. Mutual goodwill is made up of laziness, courtesy, lies, of a multitude of things that conceal the barricades from us. Even a tacit agreement involves such disagreement over details and itineraries that there is excuse enough here for us to get lost and be separated for ever. If we meet a mind that seems to us propelled by the same mechanism as our own and are amazed at its swiftness in traversing the zones with which we are concerned, we learn later that it specializes in, for example, music, and this proves what a mirage it was that seemed to bring it close to us. Sentiment has carried it far from intelligence. It is no longer in control. Some weakness, let in at an early stage, that it has every moment cajoled, fortified and worked on ever since, has ended by developing the muscles of an athlete and choking off the rest. Here is a spirit capable of understanding everything, which understands nothing. The use of what attracted us remains nil. This strong-minded individual loves bad music and devotes himself to it. Deaf to true riches he is no longer free on this vital point. Along any other path he travels with ease. An atrophied limb is the only one he uses and the melancholy sight of this atrophy fills him with pride.

Of graver import is our apparent agreement all along the line. This is what enables us to live and what art exploits in order to persuade us to serve its cause. A work of art is so intensely the expression of our solitude that one wonders what strange necessity for making contact impels an artist to expose it to the light.

A work of art, through the medium of which a man *heroically exposes* himself, perhaps quite unconsciously, evinces another form of heroism and will strike root in others by means of subterfuges comparable to those nature uses to perpetuate itself. Does a work of art hold an indispensable hierarchy, or has man, imitatively conformed in the long run to the universal methods of creation? It is certain that he is a slave to them, that, without knowing it, he clothes his creative force in decorative apparel fit to bear witness to his presence, to intrigue, to startle, to seduce, to survive at whatever cost by signals totally unconnected with its mission and by the same artifice as that of flowers.

A work of art carries its defence within itself. This is made up of numerous unconscious concessions that allow it to conquer habit and to implant itself through a misconception. Thanks to having got this hold, it clings fast and its secret seed gets to work.

An artist can expect no help from his peers. Any art form which is not his own must be intolerable to him and upsets him to the highest degree. I have seen Claude Debussy ill at the orchestral rehearsals of *Le Sacre*. His soul was discovering its splendour. The form that he had given to his soul was suffering from another that did not accord with its own contours. Therefore no help. Neither from our peers nor from a mob incapable of consenting without revolt to a violent break with the habits it had begun to form. Whence will help come? From no one. And it is then that art begins to use the obscure stratagems of nature in a kingdom which resists it, which even seems to fight it or to turn its back upon it.

I have a friend who is a typical example of this. His contribution is incalculable. His name is Jean Genêt. No one had armed himself better against contacts, no one guarded his solitude better. However, it is precisely penal servitude, eroticism, a whole new psychology, a physiological one so to speak, a whole arsenal of resistance, that earns him contact, fascinates and attracts those who appear most rebellious. For his genius projects forcefully powers which, displayed by talent, would be no more than 'picturesque'. He dumbly obeys the order to scatter his seeds. The trick has come off. Faithful to its old method, beauty dons the mask of a criminal. I ponder this before a photograph of Weidmann[4] given me by Genêt. Swathed in bandages, he is so beautiful that one wonders if crime does not employ the universal stratagem and if this is not one of its methods of luring what it kills, of exciting its converts, of exercising a sinister prestige, in short of perpetuating itself.

Is man capable of penetrating the mystery which I am analysing and of becoming its master? No, technique itself is a snare. Wilde rightly observes that technique is only individuality. The technicians, in my film *La Belle et la Bête*, credited me with first class technique. I have none. In fact there is none. Doubtless they give the name technique to the feats of equilibrium that the mind instinctively brings into play every second, so as not to break its neck. This is what Picasso's great phrase sums up: *'Le métier, c'est ce qui ne s'apprend pas.'*

But I insist. We have to live shoulder to shoulder with minds where the space separating us is gloomier than that of atoms and stars. This is of what a theatre audience, before which we brazenly expose ourselves, is composed. There is the void into which we send our poems, our drawings, our reviews. There is the park buzzing with insects intent on their food and which the world's factory employs for other ends.

For, while admitting that some of these insects might have opinions, this does not upset the rule. This rule is robust enough to stand a few exceptions. It relies on grand totals. It works wholesale. Its prodigality is dispensed with both hands. It is ignorant of the code. That a great number of its balls go astray

4 A notorious criminal of the 1930s. E.S.

matters little to it. It is rich in them. It aims to put one ball into the hole.

On customs

Writing is an act of love. If it is not it is only handwriting. It consists in obeying the driving force of plants and trees and in broadcasting sperm far around us. The richness of the world is in its wastefulness. This germinates, that falls by the wayside. Thus it is with sex. The centre of pleasure is very vague albeit very keen. It invites the race to perpetuate itself. This does not prevent it from functioning blindly. A dog espouses my leg. A bitch gets to work on a dog. A certain plant, once tall, now atrophied, still contrives a parachute for its seed that hits the ground before it can open. Women in the Pacific Islands give birth on a dung heap so that only strong children survive. From fear of over-population these islands favour what are usually considered evil practices.

Soldiers, sailors, labourers, who practise them, see no evil in them. Vice, I once wrote, begins with choice. At Villefranche in the old days I watched American sailors, for whom the practice of love assumed no precise form, and who made do with anybody or anything. The idea of vice never crossed their minds. They acted blindly. They conformed instinctively to the very confused rules of the animal and vegetable kingdom. A fruitful woman becomes misshapen with use, which proves her nobility and that it is more insane to use her in a sterile way than for a man merely to provide a luxury for the blind desires of the flesh. Such things mean little to me, but as I like the society of young people, from whom I have a great deal to learn, and as a beautiful soul is reflected in the face, the world has decided otherwise. Besides, I think that after a certain age such things are depraved, do not allow of any exchange and accordingly become ludicrous, whether it's a question of one sex or the other.

In fact I lead the life of a monk. An incomprehensible life in a life in which people think of nothing but of rubbing themselves up against one another, of seeking that kind of pleasure, if only in dancing, in imputing it to others, in considering any friendship suspect.

No matter. We should not be on show. The more mistaken people are about us, the more they envelope us in legends, the better this shelters us and teaches us to live in peace. It is enough that our own circle should hold us in esteem. What we are to other circles is nothing to us.

A lady whom I had invited to luncheon served me up such a description of myself that I rose from the table to make my apologies. 'You are sharing,' I told her, 'the meal of someone whom I do not know and whom I would not care to know.' This lady thought she was being agreeable. Doubtless my personality would have given her nothing to hold on to. She knew another, constructed from this, that and the other, which thrilled her.

Where does the sense of beauty, I mean what impels us towards beauty, have its source? Where does it begin? Where does it end? What nerve centre makes it known to us? The spontaneous use of sexuality haunts all men of stature, whether they know it or not. Michelangelo manifests this to us. Da Vinci whispers it to us. I am less intrigued by their confessions than by the innumerable signs of an order deemed a disorder, and which is not carried to the point of action. What do actions mean? They are matters for the police. They do not interest us. Picasso is an example of this order. This woman's man is a mysogynist in his works. In them he takes revenge for the domination women wield over him and for the time they filch from him. He relentlessly attacks their faces and their costumes. Man, on the other hand, he flatters and, having nothing to complain of in him, he praises him with pen and pencil.

On line

I could have something to say about any number of subjects
that occur to me. But I resist on principle. A certain preoccupation provides me with a framework, and to move out of this
would be to be lost. Where should I stop? I should be like those
painters who paint the frame (and why not the wall and the
building?) like those Hungarian gypsies who would come down
from the platform, play from table to table and who might as
well have continued in the street.

For several years I have been moving away from the novel,
in a period of interminable novels, in which the readers skip
paragraphs and can no longer enter into the adventures of others
without exhaustion.

I have always avoided surnames in my plays and almost
always in my books. They embarrass me like too pressing an
invitation to intrude among strangers. I was waiting for two
new enterprises to obsess me: that of a film in which I would
plunge into the purifying bath of childhood, that of a book such
as I should have liked to carry in my pocket when I was very
young and very much alone. I have made the film. It is *La Belle*

et la Bête. I am making the book. It is the one I am now writing.

After *Iphigenie*, Goethe declares that his work was finished and that any further ideas would be a gift of fortune. I am inclined to think I have scraped bottom and that nothing remains. All the better if I am wrong. If not, I shall feel no bitterness. For people like to say that we have run dry when they know nothing of our work. They know a fragment or two which they regard as my whole work and look out for the sequel without having to read the beginning. It will be pleasant for me to twiddle my thumbs, to see my work take root, stretch out its branches towards the sunny side and give me shade.

Now do not go imagining that the preoccupation driving me is of an aesthetic order. It is subject only to the line.

What is the line? It is life. A line should live at every point on its course in such a way that the presence of the artist makes itself felt more strongly than that of the model. The masses base their judgement upon the line of the model, without under-standing that it may disappear in favour of that of the painter, provided that his line lives a life of its own. By line I mean the permanence of personality. For the line exists no less in Renoir, in Seurat, in Bonnard, in those in whom it seems to dissolve in the touch of the brush, as in Matisse or Picasso.

With the writer the line takes precedence over the matter and the form. It runs through the words that he puts together. It sounds a continuous note, imperceptible to both ear and eye. It is, as it were, the style of the soul, and if this line ceases to have a life of its own, if it only describes an arabesque, the soul is absent and the writing dead. That is why I am for ever say-ing that the moral progress of an artist is the only progress that matters, since this line slackens as soon as the soul abates its fire. Do not confuse moral progress with morality. Moral pro-gress is but a bracing of the self.

Protecting the line becomes our therapy as soon as we feel that it is weak or when it splits like a hair in bad condition. One recognizes it even without it signifying. And if our painters were to draw a cross on a sheet of paper I am sure I could tell you who had done it. And if I half-open a book, I recognize it before it is fully open.

Faced with this revealing line, people look only at its trappings. The more visible it is the less they see it, used as they are to admiring only what adorns it. They come to prefer Ronsard to Villon, Schumann to Schubert, Monet to Cézanne.

What can they learn from Erik Satie in whom this adorable line goes naked? From Stravinsky, whose sole concern is to flay it alive?

The draperies of Beethoven and Wagner fill them with enthusiasm. They are none the less incapable of seeing the line, pronounced though it is, about which those draperies are wound.

You will tell me that a man does not display his skeleton, that this would be the direst offence against modesty. But this line is not a skeleton. It devolves from the glance, the tone of voice, the gesture, the bearing, from the whole which makes up the physical personality. It gives evidence of a motive force, over whose source and nature philosophers cannot agree.

Before a piece of music, a painting, a statue, a poem has begun to speak to us, we have already described its line. It is the line that moves us when an artist decides to break with the visible world and compels his forms to obey him.

For music, although apparently under no constraint to be representative, in fact is so, in as much as it reproduces what the composer has in mind to say. No other art form can express such nonsense or such banalities. And if the composer departs from what the ear is accustomed to, he angers the public in the same way as does the painter or the writer.

In the case of the composer, a somewhat rare phenomenon enables us to see the phantom line other than by an extra sense. This occurs when it is embodied in a melody. When a melody embraces the course of the line to the point of being integrated with it.

When I was composing *Oedipus Rex* with Stravinsky, we travelled through the Alpes-Maritimes. It was in March. The almond trees were in bloom on the mountains. One evening, when we stopped at a small inn, we counted up those melodies of *Faust* in which Gounod surpasses himself. They invoke the atmosphere of dreams. Our neighbour at the next table rose and introduced himself. He was the composer's grandson. He told us that Gounod dreamt these melodies of *Faust* and that he wrote them down on waking.

Would not this seem like the extension of faculties that allow us to fly in dreams?

It is with reference to these that Mme J.-M. Sert (most of whose words deserve to be quoted) used to say that in *Faust* one is in love and that in *Tristan* one makes love.

This ideal line retraces for us the lives of great men. It accompanies their actions and threads them together. It is, without doubt the only certainty able to withstand the false perspective of history. It leaps to the eyes of the soul before memory interferes.

Not to mention Shakespeare, an Alexandre Dumas always makes use of it. He wraps it round with his fiction and strikes us with a truth more rigid than that of a broken stick in the waters of time.

It is this line too that the graphologist is able to extract from hand-writing, whatever artifices disguise it. The more it is disguised, the clearer it becomes. For the depositions of artifice augment the exhibits in the case.

Whatever a certain kindly woman bookseller may think – she accuses me of hoisting the flag and letting others take the risks – my line is one of shocks and of risks. The lady would see, with a little thought, that her military metaphor is, to say the least, suspect. If one does not attack, how can one hoist the flag? It is precisely the fear of becoming less able to charge in this way that might make me decide to shut up shop. Even so it would be impossible for me, so long as my legs are sound, not to run towards the outposts and hang around to see what is happening.

By and large, a line of combat runs through my works. If I have ever captured the enemy's weapons, I have made them mine in battle. They are judged by the outcome. He should put them to better use.

From hopscotch to posters, I recognize nearly all the themes

Picasso adopts in the various districts he inhabits. For him they play the part of a landscape-painter's *motif*, but he takes them home, shuffles them about and raises them to the dignity of service.

When cubism was at its height, the Montparnasse painters shut themselves in for fear Picasso should pilfer some precious seed and make it bloom on his own soil. Once in 1916, when he took me to see them, I was party to an interminable confabulation on the doorstep. We had to wait until they had first hidden away their latest canvases, under lock and key. They equally mistrusted one and all.

This state of siege nourished the silences of the *Rotonde* and the *Dôme*. I remember one week when everyone there was whispering, wondering who had stolen from Rivera his trick of painting trees in dots of black and green.

The cubists did not realize, intoxicated as they were with their little discoveries, that they owed these to Picasso or to Braque who, in orchestrating them, would be merely taking back what was their own. Besides, they need not have bothered their heads, since our line does not easily assimilate a foreign form and repels what would buckle it, as one says of a wheel.

And when I speak of my borrowing weapons, I am not speaking of my writing, but of skirmishes during which a sudden volte-face enables me to turn against the enemy the weapons that he was aiming at me.

I therefore advise young people to adopt the practice of beautiful women and to *care for their line*, to prefer the lean to the fat. And not to look at themselves in a mirror, but simply to look at themselves.

On a drama in mime

Our machine disrupts itself a little more each day and each morning man wakes with a new impediment. I recognize this. I used to sleep right through the night. Now I wake up. This sickens me. I get up. I start working. It is the only means that makes it possible for me to forget my blemishes and acquire beauty at my table. This 'writing-face' being, when all is said and done, my true face. The other, a fading shadow. Quickly now let me construct my features in ink to replace those that are leaving me.

This is the face that I am trying to establish and to embellish with the spectacle of a ballet, presented last night, the 25th of June 1946, at the Théâtre des Champs-Elysées. I felt myself beautiful, thank to the dancers, to the sets, to the music, and as this result entails a deal of artifice exceeding the creator's approval, I propose to study it.

I have long been trying to make use, otherwise than in films, of the mystery of accidental synchronization. For music finds its response not only in each individual, but also in any plastic work with which it is confronted, if this work is of the same calibre. Not only is this synchronization a kind of family affair, embracing the action as a whole, but further what is more – and herein lies the mystery – it underlines its details to the great surprise of those who considered its use sacrilegious.

I already knew of this peculiarity through the experience of films, in which any music of quality integrates the gestures and emotions of the characters. It remained to prove that a dance, set to rhythms suiting the choreographer, could do without them and gain strength in a new musical climate.

Nothing is more contrary to the play of art than a redundancy of movements representing notes.

Counterpoint, the skilled unbalance from which changes are born, cannot be produced when perfect balance engenders inertia.

It is from a delicate arrangement of unbalance that balance draws its charm. A perfect face proves this when one divides it and remakes it of its two left sides. It becomes grotesque. Architects knew this long ago and in Greece, at Versailles, in Venice, in Amsterdam, one may see how the asymmetric lines make for the beauty of their buildings. The plumb-line kills this almost human beauty. One knows the flatness, the deadly boredom of our blocks of flats to which man has resigned himself.

About a month ago, at a luncheon with Christian Bérard and Boris Kochno, the trustee of Serge de Diaghilev's methods, I envisaged the possibility of a dance scene in which the dancers would practise to jazz rhythms, such rhythms considered as simple aids to work and being replaced later by some great work of Mozart, Schubert or Bach.[1]

---

[1] In the long run the line of the music and that of the dance, which contradict one another, incline towards each other and blend. Dancers who had complained of the clash but had grown accustomed to it, come to the point of complaining that there is too much accord. They ask me to change the basic music. I have decided for New York to alternate to Bach's *Passacaglia* with the Overture to Mozart's *The Magic Flute*. Thus I shall prove how far the eye takes precedence over the ear in the theatre, and that works as widely different as these can adapt themselves to the same theme. But what is done is done and my guess is that it will not now be changed. The bag is much travelled. The things in it have rubbed off their corners and sleep has relaxed their attitudes. They lazily subside.

The next day we set about carrying out this final plan. The scene would serve as a pretext for a dialogue in gestures between Mlle Philippart and M. Babilée, in whom I find much of the resilience of Vaslav Nijinsky. I decided to take a hand only in so far as to describe in detail to the scenic designer, to the costumier, to the choreographer and to the performers what I expected of them. I fixed my choice on Vakhévitch, designer, because he designs film sets and I wanted this high relief from which the cinematograph draws its dreams; on Mme Karinska, the wardrobe mistress, helped by Bérard, because they know stage optics better than anyone else; on Roland Petit, choreographer, because he would listen to me and translate me into that dance-language which I speak fairly well, but of which I lack the syntax.

The set depicts the studio of a most unhappy painter. This studio is in the form of a triangle. One of its sides would be the footlights. The apex closes the set. A post almost in the centre, a little to the right, rises from the floor, forming a gallows supporting a beam that crosses the ceiling from the prompt side to the opposite side. A rope with a slip knot hangs from the gallows and the iron framework of a lamp, wrapped in an old newspaper, dangles from the beam between the gallows and the wall on the left. Against the right wall, its dirty roughcast starred with the dates of engagements, with drawings done by me, an iron bedstead with a red blanket and sheets trailing on the floor. Against the left wall, a wash-stand of similar style. In the left foreground, a door. Between the door and the footlights a table and straw-bottomed chairs. Other chairs are strewn about. One of them just under the slip knot, near the door. A glazed skylight in the steeply sloping ceiling shows a Paris night sky. The whole thing, due to harsh lighting, long shadows, the splendour, the squalor, the dignity, the indignity, will evoke the world of Baudelaire.

Before the rise of the curtain the orchestra strikes up J. S. Bach's *Passacaglia*, orchestrated by Respighi. The curtain rises. The young painter is lying on his bed on his back, one foot raised along the wall. His head and one of his arms are hanging over the red blanket. He is smoking. He is wearing neither a

shirt nor socks, but only a wrist watch, old slippers and the kind
of boiler-suit known as '*stokers blues*', of a dark blue on which
the many coloured stains call to mind Harlequin's motley.

The first phase (for immobility plays in this solemn fugue
as active a part as motion) shows us the anguish of this young
painter, his nervous tension, his dejection, the watch he keeps
looking at, his pacing to and fro, his pauses under the rope he
has knotted to the beam, his ear hesitating between the ticking
of the time and the silence of the stairs. Mime which, carried
to excess, incites the dance. (One of the *motifs* being that magnificent, circular and airy movement of a man consulting his
wrist watch.)

The door opens. A young girl enters, a brunette, elegant,
lithe, without a hat, in a simple pale yellow dress, very short
(Gradiva's shade of yellow) and black gloves. Right from the
door, which she closes behind her, she pricks out her ill humour
on her points. The young man dashes towards her, she repels
him and strides across the room. He follows her. She upsets
some chairs. The second phase will be the dance of the painter
and this young girl who insults him, knocks him about, shrugs
her shoulders, kicks him. The scene works up to the dance, that
is to say to the uncoiling of bodies that clinch and unclinch, a
cigarette that is spat out and crushed underfoot, a girl who three
times running stamps with her heel on a poor kneeling fellow
who falls, spins round, collapses, straightens up again with the
extreme slowness of heavy smoke, in short of anger's exploding
thunderbolts.

This shifts our dancers to the extreme left of the room,
whence the unhappy young man indicates the rope with an
outstretched arm. And now the young lady cajoles him, leads
him to a seat, sets him astride it, climbs on to the chair under
the beam, adjusts the slip knot, then comes back and turns his
head towards his gallows.

The young man's revolt, his fit of fury, his chase after the
fleeing girl whom he grasps by the hair, the flight of the girl and
the door-slam that brings the second phase to an end.

The third phase shows the young man flattened against the
door. His dance proceeds from his paroxysm. One after another

he whirls the chairs in the air at arm's length and breaks them against the walls. He tries to drag the table towards the gallows, stumbles, falls, gets up again, knocks the table over with his back. He clutches his breast in pain. Cries of pain issue from his mouth, which we see but do not hear. Pain steers him straight to the gallows. He contemplates the noose. He stretches up to it. He puts it round his neck.

It is at this point that M. Babilée displays an admirable cunning. How does he hang himself? I cannot think. *He does hang himself.* He hangs. His legs hang. His arms hang. His hair hangs. His shoulders hang. The sight of this sombre poetry, accompanied by the magnificence of Bach's brass, was so beautiful that the audience broke into applause.

The fourth phase begins. The light changes. The room takes flight, leaving nothing but the triangle of the floor, the furniture, the framework of the gallows, the hanged man and the lamp.

These are now seen against the open night sky, in the midst of a surging sea made up of chimneys, of garrets, of electric signs, of rain-pipes, of roof-tops. In the distance the letters of *Citroën* light up in turn on the Eiffel Tower.

Across the roofs comes Death. She is a young white-faced woman in a ball-dress, perched on high buskins. A red hood covers her small skeleton's head. She has on long red gloves, bracelets and a diamond necklace. Her tulle train trails after her on to the stage.

Her right hand, lifted, indicates the void. She advances towards the footlights. She turns away, crosses the stage, pauses on the extreme right and snaps her fingers. Slowly the young man frees his head from the slip knot, slides along the beam and lands on the ground. Death removes her skeleton's mask and her hood. It is the yellow girl. She puts the mask on the motionless youth. He moves round her, walks a few steps, stops. Then Death holds out her hands. This gesture seems to urge on the young man with the stamp of death on his face. The *cortège* of the two dancers sets out across the roof-tops.

Yesterday the ballet company had just returned from Switzer-

land. From morning to night it was a matter of reassembling the
scattered properties of our production, of marshalling our
dances and the orchestra of sixty-four musicians, of getting the
dresses finished at Mme Karinska's, of persuading Mlle Philippart
to walk on high buskins, of fastening straps to them, of painting
M. Babilée's boiler suit, of putting up the set of the room and
the roof-tops, of fitting up the electric signs, of fixing the lighting-
plot. In short, at seven o'clock in the evening, while the stage-
hands cleared the stage, we found ourselves faced with the prospect of disaster. The choreography came to a halt with the
hanging of the young man. Roland Petit had refused to do anything about the last scene in my absence. The dancers were
half dead with exhaustion. I suggested that we should let them
sit in the auditorium and mime their parts to them. This we
did.

I returned to the Palais-Royal. I dined. At ten o'clock I was
back at the theatre where the crowd was finding no seats left,
where the box office, overwhelmed, was turning away people
who had booked theirs. Henri Sauguet had just left, furious. He
had taken his orchestral score with him. He refused to allow *Les
Forains* to be performed. The auditorium was crammed and in
a state of great nervous tension. *Le jeune homme et la mort*
was third on the bill. The set of the roof-tops presents a difficulty unusual in a ballet. The stage-hands kept losing their heads.
The audience was growing impatient, stamping its feet,
booing.

While the stage-hands went on with their work, Boris ordered
the house lights to be put out. The orchestra struck up. From the
very first chords of the Bach, we had the feeling that an extraordinary calm was pervading the whole place. The semi-dark-
ness of the wings, full of running feet, of shouted orders, of
feverish dressers (for Death had to be dressed in one minute)
was less chaotic than one would have dared hope. Suddenly I
saw Boris, looking distraught. He whispered to me : 'There's not
enough music.' That was the danger of our experiment. We
called to the dancers to quicken the pace. They were no longer
with us.

The miracle is that Boris was wrong, that the music was

long enough and that our dancers left the stage on the last chords.

I had advised them not to acknowledge the applause at the curtain call but to continue on their sleep-walkers' course.

They only came down from the roof-tops at the third curtain. And it was at the fourth that we realized that the audience was emerging from a hypnotic trance. I came to my senses on the stage, dragged forward by my dancers, facing that suddenly awakened audience, which was waking us by its uproar.

I must emphasize the fact that if I tell of this success, it is not a question of any satisfaction I derive from it, but a question of that image which every poet, young or old, beautiful or ugly, tries to substitute for his own, and to which he gives the task of embellishing it.

Let me add that one minute of contact between an audience and a work momentarily abolishes the space that separates us from other people. This phenomenon, which can centralize the most opposed electric currents at the end of some point, enables us to live in a world where the ritual of courtesy alone gives us respite from the sickening loneliness of the human being.

A *ballet* possesses, moreover, the privilege of speaking all languages and of lifting the barrier between ourselves and those who speak in tongues unknown to us.

This evening they are taking me from my country retreat to the wings from which I shall watch the second performance. When I get back, I propose to write whether the contact is broken or still holds.

I have just come back from the Champs-Elysées Theatre. Our ballet was given the same reception. Perhaps our dancers had less fire, but they performed their dances with a greater precision. In any case, whatever goes amiss, the beauty of the performance leaps the footlights, and the general atmosphere is an image of me, of my table, of my myths, an involuntary paraphrase of *Le Sang d'un poète*.

Only, from being invisible this atmosphere has become visible. This is what happens with *La Belle et la Bête*. Doubtless I am less clumsy with my guns, less hasty on the trigger. At any rate with this I reap a harvest that I failed to do in the old days with works more worthy of rousing emotion. I suppose these works fructify in silence and make the audience, without realizing it, better able to understand their content.

Thus quite a few people in 1946 thought that I had altered certain passages in *Les Parents Terribles*, whereas the play is the same as in 1939; it is they themselves who have changed, but they attribute this change to an alteration of the text.

Tonight the orchestra was ahead. It therefore came in on different movements. The synchronization worked faultlessly. The room was late in taking flight, leaving M. Babilée hanging from his beam. This produced a new beauty as a result of which the entry of Death was even more startling.

Is *Le jeune homme et la mort* a ballet? No. It is a drama in mime, in which mime broadens its style to that of the dance. It is a dumb show in which I endeavour to endow gestures with the high relief of the cry and the spoken word. It is speech translated into the language of the body. It consists of monologues and dialogues that use the same vocabulary as painting, sculpture and music.

When shall I cease to read, with reference to this work or any other, praises of my lucidity? What do our critics imagine? There is my workshop. Work goes on there at night, when all the lights are out. I simply grope about and manage as best I can. That they should mistake this obsession with work, this being haunted by work, *that is to say by a work no longer concerned for a moment with what it is manufacturing*, for lucidity, for the supervision of this workshop, where nothing is overlooked, is evidence of a basic misapprehension, a very serious divorce between the critic and the poet.

For nothing but aridity would be born of this master's eye. Whence would come the drama? Whence the dream? Whence the shadow they believe to be magic?

There is neither magic nor master's eye. Only a great deal of love and a great deal of work. On this intervention of the soul they trip up, accustomed as they are on the one hand to Voltaire's metronome, on the other to Rousseau's hazel switch. The precarious balance between these two extremes is perhaps the winning over of the modern trend, but for that critics must explore the zone, visit its mines and let in the unknown.

On responsibility

Now here is this weird sensation of deadlock beginning to grip me at the four cardinal points of my system and to knot itself at the centre. Is it the sudden heat or the storm, or the loneliness, or the uncertainty over the dates for my play, or the prospect of being homeless, or is it simply that this book refuses to go any further? I know these attacks of vague anguish, having often been their victim. Nothing is harder than to give them a shape that will allow us to look them in the face. From the moment this *malaise* appears, it dominates us. It does not allow us to read, write, sleep, walk, to live. It surrounds us with obscure threats. All that was opening closes. All that was helping deserts us. All that smiled looks on us icily. We dare not take a step. The ventures suggested to us wilt, become entangled, capsize over one another. Each time I let myself be caught by these advances of fate, which only lure us on the better to desert us. Each time I tell myself that I have reached calm waters, that I have paid dearly enough for the right to descend a gentle slope, and no longer slide headlong in the night.

No sooner am I lulled by this illusion than my body calls me to order. It switches on one of those red lights signifying *Danger*. Sufferings that I believed to have disappeared return with the anger of those who have made a false exit and bear us a further grudge for having appeared ridiculous. My eyelids, my temples, my neck, my chest, my shoulders, my arms, my knuckles, devour me. The Morzine farce begins again. I get better and the malady thereby gains strength. It even seems to want to attack my mucous membrane, my gums, my throat, my palate. From the works it passes into the fuel and pollutes it. Patches of irritation, gum-boils of misery, fevers of despair, fill us with slight but most distressing symptoms. They grow quickly into a kind of nausea that we attribute to outside influence. It is probably our own condition colouring the world and making us think it responsible for our own colour. This jiggery-pokery only messes up my outside and my inside still further. Life appears to us insoluble, too vast, too small, too long, too short. Once, as a palliative for these constantly recurring attacks, I used to take opium, a remedy inducing euphoria. I gave it up ten years ago, on account of an honesty which is perhaps only foolishness. I wished to rely on my own resources alone, which does not make sense, since our inner self is made up of what we feed upon. In short, nothing is left to me but to endure these attacks and wait for the outcome.

The one inhabiting me since yesterday announced itself a fortnight ago by a fresh outbreak of my ills. I should like to consider the sultry heat turning to thunder an additional factor. For the last five minutes it has been blowing and raining. I remember a paragraph in Michelet's *l'Histoire* in which he congratulates himself on being untroubled by the squalls beating against his window. On the contrary he derived comfort from them and observed in them the rhythm of nature. These squalls held for him a promise of fine weather. What fine weather? I wonder. I should like to be my own tuner and tighten up my nerves to my own pitch when heat or frost have sent me out of tune. What am I saying? The slightest moral dampness, the slightest mental feverishness.

Should one envy those great ogres like Goethe or like Hugo in whom egoism passes for heroism and who manage to make people admire such monstrous sayings as: '*Par-dessus les tombes, en avant*'? It is thus that Goethe receives the news of his son's death. What matters whether we envy them or do not envy them? The die is cast. And I add nothing to my glory nor to theirs by being cast in one mould or another.

But I assure you that it is the way I am made that I have to thank for being a rolling stone. The place I hoped for and in which I hide quickly becomes a trap. I escape from it and thus it goes on. I have only to discover a place of retreat, for everything to conspire against me and prevent me from signing the contract.

Nothing is so rigid as this rhythm that bears us along and that we imagine to be under our control. Its impetus deceives us. Failure is masked by it. It never shows itself twice with the same face. However much we expect it, we do not recognize it.

Has the book I am writing completed its curve? I who boast, and in these very chapters, that I never worry about this and that I am never warned of it except by a sudden shock, now, for the first time, am questioning myself. Shall I be able to go on talking to you always and keeping this journal – which, as is the way of journals, is not one – based on what happens to me? It would be to tamper with its mechanism. It would be not to write the book that comes to me, but another one which I would be forcing. I surrender to the trickery of a station platform where one runs the length of the train, where one jumps on to the footboard, where one tries to delay the breaking of the thread wound round one's own heart and that of those who are departing. I find myself torn between my taste for regular habits and the fatality that compels me to break them. I had come to imagine us so clearly, youth matching my youth, standing at a street corner, sitting in a square, lying face down on a bed, elbows on a table, gossiping together. And I leave you. Without leaving you, needless to say, since I am so closely merged with my ink that my pulse beats into it. Do you not feel it under your thumb, as it holds the corner of the pages? That would astonish me, since it throbs under my pen and produces that inimitable, wild, nocturnal, ultra-complex hubbub of my heart, recorded in *Le Sang d'un Poète*. 'The poet is dead. Long

live the poet.' This is the cry of his ink. This is what his muffled
drums beat out. This is what lights his funeral candelabra. This
is what shakes the pocket in which you put my book and makes
passers-by turn their heads and wonder what the noise is. This
is the whole difference between a book that is simply a book
and this book which is a person changed into a book. Changed
into a book and crying out for help, for the spell to be broken
and he reincarnated in the person of the reader. This is the
sleight-of-hand I ask of you. Please understand me. It is not so
difficult as it seems at first sight.

You take this book out of your pocket. You read. And if
you manage to read it without anything being able to distract
you from my writing, little by little you will feel that I inhabit
you and you will resurrect me. You may even chance to use a
gesture of mine, a glance of mine. Naturally I am addressing
the youth of a period when I shall no longer be there in flesh
and bone nor my blood mingled with my ink.

We are in full agreement. Do not forget that my pen strokes,
now become printed letters, must reform in you their convolutions
momentarily entwining your line with mine, to such a degree
as to ensure an exchange of warmth between us.

If you follow my instructions to the letter, the phenomenon
of osmosis will occur, owing to which this somewhat noxious
parcel, which is a book, ceases to be so, thanks to a pact of
mutual assistance by which the living help the dead and the
dead help the living. Let us say no more about it.

This evening, while addressing the children of our children's
children, I am suffering from a pretty unpleasant complaint.
Between the middle and ring finger of my right hand
the skin is peeling. Under my arms there are clumps of nettles.
I force myself to write, because idleness increases my torture
tenfold. And that is why I project myself into a time when
it will be my pages' turn to suffer. Which they may perhaps do. For ink as persuasive as mine can never be quite at
peace.

Oh how I should love to be well! To produce plays, films,
poems by the armful. So to toughen the flesh of my paper that
pain could not get its teeth into it.

And how I complained! Of what? Of influenza. Of neuritis. Of typhoid. Of a fair duel with death. I was forgetting that insidious ailment that destroys us just as man destroys the earth, laboriously. The stealthy strike in my factory. The broken parts than cannot be replaced. I was forgetting my age, that is all there is to it.

Jean Genêt, who must surely be regarded as a moralist one day, paradoxical as this may seem, since we are in the habit of confusing the moralist with the moralizer, a few weeks ago said these poignant words to me: 'To watch our heroes live and to pity them is not enough. We must take their sins upon ourselves and suffer the consequences.'

Who are my real heroes? Emotions. Abstract figures who none the less live and whose demands are exacting. This is what I came to understand when listening to Genêt and noting the ravages wrought in his soul by the crimes of *l'Egyptien Querelle*.[1] He knew himself to be responsible and rejected any plea of irresponsibility. He was ready, not to consider an action being brought against the effrontery of his book, but to endorse any action which a higher court might bring against his characters.[2]

At one stroke he throws a great light for me over the endless trial in which I find myself involved. At one stroke he explains to me the reason why I experience no sense of revolt. In this indictment bearing on words, attitudes, hallucinations, it is right for the author to accept responsibility and to appear at the bar between two policemen. It is out of the question for an author to judge, to have a seat on the bench at his own trial and incline to compassion for the guilty. A man is on one side or the other of the bar. This is the very basis of our commitment.

Were I not of the breed that is always accused and ill-equipped for defence, what shame I should have felt before Genêt when he confided to me the secret of his torment. For

---

[1] Refers to *Querelle de Brest* by Jean Genêt. E.S.

[2] In order to 'place' Jean Genêt in the eyes of the Court of Justice (1942) I told this Court that I considered him to be one of France's great writers. One can guess how the newspapers under the Occupation gloated over the whole business. But a Paris Court is always afraid of repeating some famous blunder, of condemning Baudelaire. I saved Genêt. And I do not withdraw any of my evidence.

that matter, would he have confided it to me had he not recognized me, long ago and at first sight, by those signs which enable outlaws to recognize one another? I had seen Genêt refuse to be introduced to a famous writer whose immorality *appeared to him suspect*.

It is essential that I should state openly in advance that I stand by my own ideas, however contradictory they may be, and that mankind's Court of Justice can charge nobody but me. They take shape, I repeat, as characters. They take action. I alone am responsible for their actions. I should be ashamed to say, like Goethe, after the suicides brought about by *Werther*: 'This is no concern of mine.'

It is therefore natural that I should shoulder the judicial errors to which ideas, easy to distort and without an alibi, will always give rise.[3]

I do not for a moment conceal from myself the terrible harm that a witty lawyer, a witness for the prosecution, and the distance that separates the jury from a poet, can do to my work through my personality. I exonerate them, far-fetched though the verdict may be. It would be too simple if one could move around with impunity ignoring laws in a world regulated by them.[4]

5 July 1946

[3] It sometimes happens in this world that public judicial redress is made. Condemned for incest in 1939 by the Municipal Council and in 1941 by the Militia, the mother and the son in *Les Parents Terribles,* perfectly pure and childlike, were unanimously acquitted as a result of an appeal in 1946.

[4] I know very well what will be said about this book. The author's preoccupation with himself is exasperating. Who is not thus preoccupied? The critics to begin with, who no longer judge objectively, but only in relation to themselves. A phenomenon in an age in league against the individual, who in consequence will only individualize himself further, in that spirit of contradiction that makes the world go round and particularly France.

Postscript

Here you are then, cured and intrepid. Intrepid and stupid, tossed about in the confusion you abhor, always in flight from something, flying towards something, your sledge surrounded with snow and with wolves on your track.

Here you are, cured and alone, returning to winter in this big empty house where you were writing this book, with a family around you. You were writing this book, whose first proofs you are correcting, of which you now understand next to nothing.

Intrepid and stupid, encumbered with tasks that lead you into more tasks, trying to reach a target that you decorate like a Christmas tree.

Have you any right to Christmas and to a quiet home? Have you any right to pen these quiet works that judge men and condemn them to death?

The other evening, during a conversation at table, you discovered how old you were. You did not even know that, because you cannot count properly and you did not in any way connect the date of your birth and the year we have reached. Something in you was dumbfounded. This something spread perniciously through your whole system until you said to yourself: 'I am old.' You would doubtless have preferred to hear yourself say: 'You are young', and to believe what flatterers tell you.

Intrepid and stupid you should have made up your mind. This limits the difficulty of being, since for those who embrace a cause, anything outside it is non-existent.

But all causes appeal to you. You have not wished to deny yourself a single one. You have chosen to slip between them all and get the sledge through.

Right then, intrepid spirit, straighten yourself out! Forward, intrepid and stupid! Run the risk of being to the very end.

Note

Written after 'The Eagle with Two Heads'.

I had decided (something within me to be precise had decided) to embark on a work in which psychology would in a way be absent. Psychology proper would give place to an heroic or heraldic psychology. To put it plainly the psychology of our heroes would bear as little relation to real psychology as do unicorns and lions in tapestries to real animals. Their behaviour (lions' laughter, unicorns carrying banners) would belong to the theatre as these fabulous beasts belong to a coat of arms. Such a work had, of its nature, to be invisible, illegible in short to psychologists. To make it visible I needed sets, costumes, Edwige Feuillière and Jean Marais. That is to say the colour and fragrance of flowers. This was necessary for the organic vegetation of the work so that the carriers – I mean the audience – should spread my pollen.

Art is worthless in my opinion unless it be the projection of some ethic. All else is decoration. It is right to regard a work as decorative if this is lacking, in an age when decoration seduces both the eye and the ear.

Rimbaud has drained the theme of the written curse to the very dregs. The curse (which solitude and state of health should be called), must then lose the attributes that made it recognizable at first glance, and present the artist with the false attitude it entails, in a new form.

Success and lack of success can serve our loneliness in the same way. The age we live in settles the matter and compels us instinctively to protect ourselves from respect, whether by apparent failure, or by an appearance of success.

Since the chapters of this book were written and printed, *l'Aigle à deux têtes* has been produced in the theatre. I made no mistake in the preface, written at the same time as the play. In it I was carrying out a policy similar to that of *La Belle et la Bête*. A policy comparable with that of an age in which policies and wars played no part, in which our spiritual differences were the only valid policy. (The surrealists and myself for example.)

The success of the play (due to colour and atmosphere superficial to the work but which draw the public) stands in opposition to all critical judgment solely concerned with art and a prey to habit.

It must be fully understood that art, I say so once more, does not exist *qua* art, pure and simple, detached, free, rid of its creator, but is born only of his cry, his laughter, his grief. That is why certain canvases in museums beckon to me and are alive with anguish, while others are dead and present us with nothing but the embalmed corpses of Egypt.

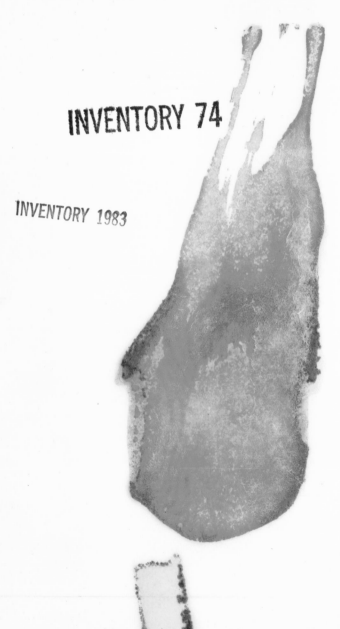